# VEGAN

# FOOD52

# VEGAN

## 60 VEGETABLE-DRIVEN RECIPES FOR ANY KITCHEN

Gena Hamshaw

Photography by James Ransom

TEN SPEED PRESS
Berkeley

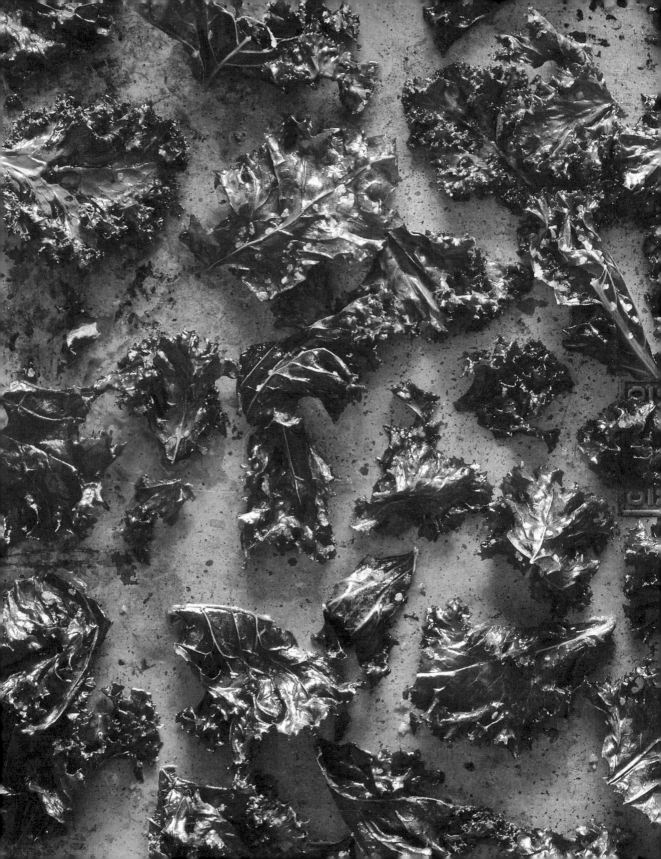

# Contents

# Foreword

When it comes to cooking and eating, we subscribe to the credo of "eat everything, and in moderation." And if we're being honest, we tend to bristle at any regimen that hinges on the rejection of an entire class—or classes—of food. Part of this is due to our upbringing, part to our past experiences as adventurous eaters and food writers, and part to our beliefs about what it means to eat healthily.

They say that as you get older you become more strident in your convictions, but we like to think this is an area where we've loosened up a little. In particular, we were wary of vegan cooking until not too long ago. When Gena's column, the New Veganism, first launched on Food52.com in 2012, it was with a primer on veganism and an accompanying recipe for raw kale salad with lentils and apricot vinaigrette.

Clean and almost spare, Gena's style ran in complete opposition to the loving embrace we gave to cream and butter and crème fraîche—not to mention steak—for so long. And this was a stance that our audience loved us for, so we were unsure of how our readers would take a vegan column.

But Gena's tolerant and graceful presentation of vegan cooking (and her use of real, seasonal ingredients) made converts of us all, and the column became one of our most widely read. This proved that our readers, like us, were not only willing but eager to let go of their preconceived notions and come along for the ride—whether they ate vegan all the time, or only for Meatless Mondays, or just liked eating more vegetable-driven dishes (or just more of Gena's dishes, because they're great).

We love that Gena's angle isn't always "look, you can make this, and it's vegan." Her column champions the enthusiasm shared by the entire Food52 community for the act of coming together around food and cooking. And she has an innate sense of what people actually want to eat.

Gena's recipes are often standouts at our photo shoots. Her Date Nut Bread (page 11) was a hot topic in the office for days; other team favorites from the book include Sweet Potato and Peanut Stew with Kale (page 54), Chilled Cucumber Soup with Mango Salsa (page 46), Roasted Ratatouille (page 101), and her Go-To Pancakes (page 8).

Even our most skeptical editors have now become the sort of people who keep a block of tofu in their fridges at all times—although that fridge may also contain anchovies or bacon or cheese or eggs. Or all five at once.

Over time, Gena has introduced us to things like nutritional yeast and cashew cheese and made them feel like new, exciting additions to our kitchens, rather than weird vegan substitutions. She was the first person to write about tempeh on the site. And now it's not so weird anymore.

Eating vegan is, at its best, less a rejection of certain foods and more an embrace of foods that are bright and flavorful—as a bonus, they're simply healthy for you, too. As Gena shows us, challenging yourself to think more expansively about these ingredients is gratifying for any cook, and will forever change the landscape of your kitchen.

—Amanda Hesser & Merrill Stubbs

# Introduction

At its heart, vegan food is just *food*. In the last few years, veganism has emerged from the "special diet" shadows and begun to take a rightful place on a wide range of dinner tables. The idea that vegan dishes belong in a separate caste—a caste populated by strange specialty ingredients, meat substitutes, and bland flavors—simply isn't true. If you like stir-fried brown rice and hearty curries at dinner, quinoa salads at lunch, or a stack of fluffy pancakes in the morning, then you already know and love vegan food. It is creative, satisfying, and colorful, and it offers tremendous possibility to the home cook.

This is the premise on which my New Veganism column on Food52 was built—the idea that vegan cuisine can be celebrated not as a set of replacements or alternatives, but as an assemblage of vibrant recipes that happen to exclude animal products. Since I started writing it two years ago, the New Veganism column has presented bold pasta dishes, hearty stews, ingenious bean burgers, nourishing whole grains, innovative salads, and rich desserts. The recipes are appealing because they're good food, plain and simple, not because they fit a label. The column also explains techniques that are helpful to vegan cooks and omnivores alike, such as making cashew cream for rich, dairy-free soups and pasta sauces; using nutritional yeast to add umami to fresh pesto; or adding avocado to smoothies for a rich, creamy texture.

This book expands upon the column that inspired it. It's a celebration of the culinary versatility of plant foods: vegetables, fruits, grains, legumes, nuts, and seeds. The recipes I share are modern and bright. The food will be light and fresh, but it won't feel like "health food" (though it is, of course, healthful). This is food you can make for yourself or share with friends and family. And it's food that you and your loved ones will relish eating.

In these pages, you'll find sixty recipes, along with many "kitchen confidence tips"—little tidbits of guidance that can help you become more adept and skillful at preparing dishes free of meat, eggs, and dairy products. I hope the book will enrich your meatless repertoire and spark—or rekindle—a love affair with vegetables.

Enjoy!

# Vegan 101

Throughout this book, you'll find occasional tidbits and tips at the end of the recipes. Taken together, these notes serve as my "Vegan 101" intro course—they are the essential techniques and insider knowledge that I think you'll need to become a more confident vegan cook. These tips cover everything from ingredient sourcing to cooking methods, and my hope is that they'll complement and enhance the recipes.

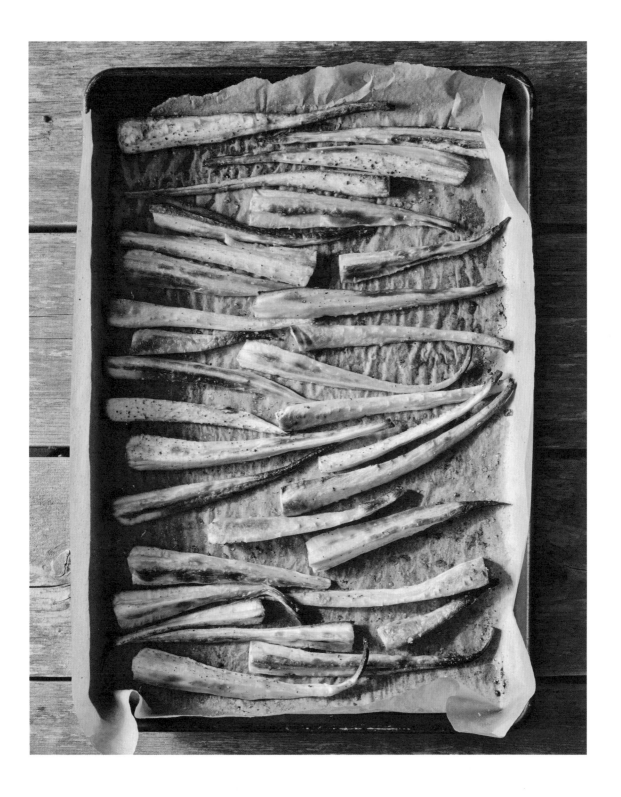

# Breakfast

# Muesli

SERVES 4

2 cups (180g) rolled oats

⅓ cup (50g) chopped medjool dates or raisins

¼ cup (30g) cashew pieces

¼ cup (35g) pumpkin seeds

3 tablespoons chia seeds

½ teaspoon ground cinnamon

¼ teaspoon ground nutmeg

3½ cups (830ml) nondairy milk, homemade (pages 133 and 134) or store-bought

2 tablespoons maple syrup, plus more if desired

With just a little advance thought, this can be a terrific grab-and-go breakfast for mornings when you simply don't have time to simmer oats but still crave a hearty bowl of cereal. A combination of oats, dates, nuts, seeds, and spices is soaked in nondairy milk overnight in the fridge, and by morning—voilà!—it's creamy, sweet, and ready to eat. You can use a variety of nuts, seeds, and dried fruits here; don't feel obliged to stick to the suggested mix-ins. This is also a great vehicle for homemade almond, rice, or oat milk, but it's fine to use your favorite store-bought in the recipe, too.

1. In a large bowl, preferably one with a lid, stir together all the ingredients. Let sit for about 20 minutes, then give it another stir. Cover and refrigerate overnight.

2. In the morning, stir again and add more nondairy milk if necessary to achieve the desired consistency. Taste for sweetness and add more maple syrup if you wish.

3. Enjoy!

# Coconut Quinoa Porridge with Toasted Almonds

SERVES 4

1 cup (170g) quinoa

1 cup (240ml) water

1½ cups (355ml) full-fat coconut milk

2 tablespoons maple syrup

¼ teaspoon salt

1 cinnamon stick, or 1 teaspoon ground cinnamon

½ cup (55g) slivered almonds

Finely chopped pitted dates (optional)

If you're an oatmeal fan, it's time to start considering breakfast porridges made with other grains. Rice, millet, quinoa, bulgur, kasha, and even farro (an ancient variety of wheat) all make for delicious morning bowls. Quinoa is a particularly convenient choice because it cooks up quickly. This porridge, which includes coconut milk, dates, and toasted almonds, has just the right amount of sweetness and a bit of crunch that nicely contrasts with the fluffiness of the quinoa. Feel free to jazz it up as you wish: almond milk, dried figs, raisins, walnuts, or chopped apple would all be good.

1. Put the quinoa in a fine-mesh sieve and rinse until the water runs clear. Combine the quinoa, water, 1 cup (240ml) of the coconut milk, and the maple syrup, salt, and cinnamon in a medium saucepan over medium-high heat. Bring to a boil, then decrease the heat to maintain a simmer, cover, and cook for about 20 minutes, until the quinoa has absorbed all the liquid. Fluff the quinoa with a fork and discard the cinnamon stick.

2. Meanwhile, toast the almonds. Put them in a small dry skillet over medium heat and cook, stirring occasionally, until golden. Immediately transfer to a plate to keep them from burning.

3. Serve right away, topping each serving with about 2 tablespoons of the remaining coconut milk, 2 tablespoons of the almonds, and a sprinkling of dates.

# Green Smoothie with Avocado

SERVES 1

1 peeled and frozen banana

½ cup (about 85g) frozen or fresh mango chunks

½ small to medium avocado

1 cup (30g) loosely packed baby spinach leaves

1½ cups (355ml) nondairy milk, homemade (pages 133 and 134) or store-bought, plus more if needed

½ teaspoon vanilla extract

The wide world of smoothies extends far beyond strawberries and bananas. Once you've experienced the fun of adding fresh leafy greens, avocado, and other unusual ingredients to your smoothies, you may find it hard to go back to your old routines. Plus, they're a no-brainer vegan breakfast. Many smoothies are dairy-free as written, and if they aren't, it's easy to veganize them using plant-based milks and yogurts in place of dairy products. This one features the sweetness of mango and a silky, almost fluffy texture thanks to the avocado.

1. Put all the ingredients in a blender and process until very smooth and creamy.

2. Add a little more nondairy milk if needed to achieve the desired consistency, or a few ice cubes if you want it to be frostier.

### Going (Frozen) Bananas

If you're a smoothie lover (and who isn't?), then it's worthwhile to keep a bag of peeled, chopped bananas in your freezer. As soon as I see a banana going ripe on my counter, I peel it and add it to my stash. They make it easy to whip up perfectly cool, thick smoothies at a moment's notice, and they're essential for achieving the creaminess of a yogurt-based smoothie.

# Go-To Pancakes

MAKES 12 TO 14 PANCAKES

2 cups (250g) unbleached all-purpose flour

2 tablespoons sugar

1 tablespoon baking powder

½ teaspoon salt

2¼ cups (530ml) unsweetened nondairy milk, homemade (pages 133 and 134) or store-bought, plus more if needed

1 teaspoon apple cider vinegar

3 tablespoons melted coconut oil, plus more for frying

1 teaspoon vanilla extract

This is my go-to pancake recipe, which also happens to turn into excellent waffles. It's sweet but not sugary and has just the slightest hint of buttery flavor from the coconut oil. The pancakes are delicious as is, and when served with maple syrup or fruit compote, but if you're looking to switch things up, try the variations that follow the recipe.

To make waffles instead of pancakes, prepare the batter as instructed, then use about ⅓ cup (80ml) of batter for each waffle.

---

1. In a large bowl, whisk together the flour, sugar, baking powder, and salt. In a medium bowl, whisk together the nondairy milk and vinegar until frothy. Stir in the coconut oil and vanilla. Add to the flour mixture and stir until smooth, taking care to break up any lumps. If the batter seems too thick, stir in a bit more nondairy milk to achieve a pourable consistency.

2. Put a griddle over medium-high heat and coat it lightly with coconut oil. When the griddle is hot, pour the pancake batter onto the griddle, using ¼ cup (60ml) for each pancake. When bubbles form on top of a pancake and the bottom is golden, flip, then cook until the other side is golden. Repeat until the batter is used up.

## For Something Different

**Pumpkin Pancakes** Use only 2 cups (475ml) of nondairy milk and whisk 1 cup (245g) of pumpkin puree into the milk mixture.

**Banana Walnut Pancakes** Use only 2 cups (475ml) of nondairy milk and whisk 1 mashed banana into the milk mixture. Fold ⅓ cup (40g) of chopped walnuts into the final batter.

**Chocolate Chip Pancakes** Fold ⅔ cup (115g) of chocolate chips into the final batter.

# Date Nut Bread

SERVES 8 TO 10

2 cups (475ml) boiling water

1½ cups (375g) pitted medjool dates, finely chopped

2 cups (250g) unbleached all-purpose flour

⅔ cup (135g) sugar

1 tablespoon baking soda

¼ teaspoon salt

1 teaspoon ground cinnamon

3 tablespoons warm water

1 tablespoon ground flaxseeds

¾ cup unsweetened nondairy milk, homemade (pages 133 and 134) or store-bought, plus more if needed

1 teaspoon apple cider vinegar

½ cup (120ml) melted coconut oil

½ cup (50g) walnuts, chopped

Soaking dates in boiling water softens them and makes them melt when baked. In this quick bread, they turn into caramel-like ribbons of sweetness. To create some binding without eggs, this recipe uses a "flax egg"—ground flaxseeds mixed with a bit of water—a handy trick of the vegan baking trade (see page 133).

1. Preheat the oven to 350°F (175°C). Oil a 5 by 9-inch (13 by 23cm) loaf pan.

2. Pour the boiling water over the dates and let soak for at least 10 minutes.

3. In a large bowl, whisk together the flour, sugar, baking soda, salt, and cinnamon.

4. In a small bowl or measuring cup, whisk together the warm water and ground flaxseeds and let sit until thick. Separately, vigorously whisk together the nondairy milk and vinegar until frothy. Add the coconut oil and the flaxseed mixture. Pour into the flour mixture and stir just until combined.

5. Drain the dates well. Fold the dates and walnuts into the batter, then stir in a splash more nondairy milk if it seems too dry. Pour the batter into the prepared pan.

6. Bake for 35 to 40 minutes, until a toothpick inserted into the center comes out clean. Let cool in the pan for 30 minutes, or until slightly warm or room temperature, then turn out onto a wire rack and let cool for at least 15 minutes longer before slicing and serving.

## Coconut Oil: The Vegan Baking All-Star

One of the first things you may be wondering as you explore vegan baking is how to replace butter. Earth Balance is the most popular brand of buttery dairy-free products, and their products are fabulous. However, coconut oil can also be used in virtually any recipe that would traditionally call for butter, with perfect results every time. If the recipe you're adapting calls for solid butter, store the coconut oil at a cool temperature. If the recipe calls for melted butter (or oil), melt the coconut oil prior to using.

# Peach Crumble Coffee Cake

SERVES 9 TO 12

### Cake

1¼ cups (155g) unbleached all-purpose flour

1 teaspoon baking powder

1 teaspoon baking soda

¼ teaspoon salt

1 teaspoon ground cinnamon

1 cup (240ml) unsweetened almond milk, homemade (page 134) or store-bought, plus more if needed

1 teaspoon apple cider vinegar

½ cup (100g) sugar

⅓ cup (80ml) melted coconut oil

1 teaspoon vanilla extract

1 cup (155g) peeled and diced ripe peaches or thawed frozen peaches

### Topping

¾ cup (95g) unbleached all-purpose flour

⅓ cup (75g) packed brown sugar

⅓ cup (35g) walnuts, chopped

⅛ teaspoon salt

1 teaspoon ground cinnamon

½ teaspoon ground ginger

4 to 5 tablespoons (60 to 75ml) melted coconut oil

This is everything a coffee cake should be: sweet, fragrant, and full of texture. There's a perfect balance among the soft, fluffy cake; the moist peaches; and the nutty, crumbly topping, which you can use on any number of cobblers, crumbles, muffins, or quick breads. It's wonderful as a breakfast treat, but it's also pretty great for dessert, especially if you top it with a scoop of vanilla ice cream.

1. Preheat the oven to 350°F (175°C). Lightly oil an 8- or 9-inch (20 or 23cm) square baking pan.

2. To make the cake, put the flour, baking powder, baking soda, salt, and cinnamon in a large bowl and whisk to combine.

3. In a medium bowl, vigorously whisk together the almond milk and vinegar until frothy. Let sit for a few moments, then stir in the sugar, coconut oil, and vanilla. Add to the flour mixture and stir just until combined, adding a little more almond milk if necessary. Fold in the peaches. Pour the batter into the prepared pan.

4. To make the topping, put the flour, sugar, walnuts, salt, cinnamon, and ginger in a small bowl and stir well. Drizzle the oil over the flour mixture, 1 tablespoon at a time, working it in with your fingers after each addition. Stop adding the oil when large crumbs form. If you like, you can also pulse the topping ingredients together in a food processor, also adding the oil 1 tablespoon at a time. Scatter the topping evenly over the batter.

5. Bake for 35 to 40 minutes, until the topping is fragrant and toasty and a toothpick inserted into the center of the cake comes out clean. Allow the cake to cool in the pan for at least 30 minutes before slicing and serving.

# Tempeh and Sweet Potato Hash

SERVES 4

2 medium to large sweet potatoes

2 tablespoons olive oil

1 cup (160g) diced onion

8 ounces (225g) tempeh, cut into squares ¾ to 1 inch (2 to 2.5cm) thick

1 teaspoon ground turmeric

1 teaspoon smoked paprika

¼ cup (60ml) vegetable broth

1 tablespoon tamari

2 teaspoons Dijon mustard

2 cups (about 150g) tightly packed chopped kale, Swiss chard, or collard greens

Pinch of red pepper flakes

Salt and pepper

One of my weekend rituals is to bake a few sweet potatoes so I can enjoy them in salads and stir-fries through the week—or in this recipe, which is a perfect vehicle for them. (That said, you could also peel, cube, and steam the sweet potatoes instead of baking them for this recipe.) Feel free to use different greens depending on the season or what looks most appealing at the market. As for the seared and spiced tempeh, it's hearty enough to sustain you on even the longest of days and pulls in some of my favorite seasonings: turmeric, tamari, and smoked paprika.

1. Preheat the oven to 400°F (200°C).

2. Pierce the sweet potatoes a few times with a fork and put them on a baking sheet. Bake for 35 to 45 minutes, until tender but not mushy. Let cool for 15 minutes.

3. Chop the sweet potatoes into ½-inch (1.3cm) cubes. Heat the olive oil in a large skillet over medium-high heat. Add the onion and sauté until the onion is just turning golden, 5 to 8 minutes. Add the tempeh and sauté until it's golden brown, 7 to 8 minutes.

4. Add the sweet potatoes, turmeric, paprika, broth, tamari, and mustard, then use the mixing spoon to mash the potatoes a bit and mix all the ingredients together. Add the greens and cook, stirring occasionally, until they wilt. Stir in the red pepper flakes and season with salt and pepper to taste. Serve right away.

## A Tempeh Tutorial

Tempeh, like tofu, is a soy product, which in this case is prepared by fermenting cakes of coarsely ground soybeans. Some varieties are made with other beans or grains in addition to soybeans. Because the fermentation process uses a fungus, you may see small gray or blackish patches. These are just spores, and they're fine. However, if you see large black or green spots, be wary; this indicates that the tempeh has spoiled. Tempeh tastes bitter unless it's been cooked, so I don't recommend eating it directly from the package. If you find it bitter even after cooking, try steaming it gently before grilling or sautéing it.

# Tofu Scramble

SERVES 4

1 tablespoon olive oil

1 cup (160g) diced onion

1 clove garlic, minced

2 cups (475ml) diced vegetables, such as zucchini and red bell peppers

2 tablespoons tahini

1 tablespoon tamari

1 tablespoon Dijon mustard

½ teaspoon ground turmeric

14 to 16 ounces (400 to 450g) extra-firm tofu, crumbled

¼ cup (20g) large-flake nutritional yeast

3 cups (90g) baby spinach or other greens, such as chard or kale

¼ cup (10g) minced fresh parsley

Pepper

I'm not particularly keen on creating "faux" versions of nonvegan dishes. But every now and then there's one that I'm dying to replicate with plant-based ingredients, this recipe being a prime example. Extra-firm tofu, crumbled and stir-fried, is an amazingly authentic substitution for scrambled eggs, especially with turmeric to give it a golden color. You can customize this recipe in all the same ways as egg-based scrambles. I like to top it with smoky-flavored tempeh strips (see page 94) for extra flavor and texture contrast, or wrap it up in a tortilla for an easy breakfast burrito.

---

1. Heat the oil a large skillet over medium heat. Add the onion and sauté until tender, 5 to 6 minutes. Add the garlic and sauté for 2 minutes. Add the vegetables and sauté until tender.

2. In a small bowl, whisk together the tahini, tamari, mustard, and turmeric. Add to the skillet and stir to combine, then stir in the tofu. Cook, stirring frequently, until the tofu is heated through, about 4 minutes. Sprinkle the nutritional yeast over the top and stir it in. Add the spinach and cook, stirring frequently, just until wilted.

3. Serve topped with the parsley and a few grinds of pepper.

### Choosing the Right Tofu For the Job

There are many types of tofu available, and it's important to select one suited to the recipe you're making. Extra-firm or firm tofu is perfect for marinating, grilling, or scrambling, or for making Tofu Feta (page 136). If marinating tofu or using it in large pieces, you'll achieve the best results if you press it first (see page 137). Silken tofu, which comes in shelf-stable boxes, is ideal for puddings, custardy pie fillings, smoothies, and creamy sauces, such as in Orecchiette with Creamy Leeks and Broccoli Rabe (page 82).

# Polenta with Greens, Roasted Tomatoes, and Lentil Walnut Crumble

SERVES 4

### Lentil Walnut Crumble
1 cup (100g) toasted walnuts

½ cup (55g) oil-packed sun-dried tomatoes, drained and coarsely chopped

1 clove garlic, chopped

1 tablespoon tamari

1 teaspoon apple cider vinegar

1 cup (200g) cooked brown lentils (see page 71)

### Roasted Tomatoes
6 Roma tomatoes, halved

2 tablespoons olive oil

1 tablespoon balsamic vinegar

2 teaspoons sugar

Salt and pepper

### Polenta
3 cups (710ml) vegetable broth

1 cup (125g) yellow cornmeal

3 tablespoons large-flake nutritional yeast

2 tablespoons olive oil

Salt and pepper

### Greens
1 tablespoon olive oil

1 clove garlic, minced

1 bunch kale or collard greens (12 to 16 ounces/340 to 450g)

1 teaspoon freshly squeezed lemon juice

Polenta is a great, savory alternative to oatmeal, and a handy opportunity to polish off leftover roasted vegetables, cooked greens, and beans. Prepare a large batch at the start of the week and reheat it in individual portions as the week goes on, adding a splash of almond milk before serving.

You can make the lentil walnut crumble in advance (stored in the fridge, it will keep for 1 week) and roast the tomatoes a day ahead. The crumble can be stuffed into wraps or used in place of crumbled tofu in a pinch.

1. Preheat the oven to 450°F (230°C).

2. To make the crumble, put the walnuts in a food processor and pulse two or three times to coarsely chop. Add the sun-dried tomatoes, garlic, tamari, and vinegar and pulse two or three more times. Add the lentils and pulse until the mixture is thoroughly blended and crumbly, adding water a teaspoonful at a time to just barely bring the ingredients together.

3. To make the roasted tomatoes, put the tomatoes, cut side up, on an oiled baking sheet and drizzle the olive oil and balsamic vinegar evenly over them. Sprinkle evenly with the sugar, then season with salt and pepper. Bake for 25 to 30 minutes, until the tomatoes are collapsing and starting to brown.

4. Meanwhile, prepare the polenta. Put the vegetable broth in a deep saucepan and bring to a boil over medium-high heat. Add the cornmeal in a thin stream while whisking. Adjust the heat to maintain a simmer. Cook, whisking constantly, until the mixture thickens, then switch to a wooden spoon and cook, stirring constantly, until thick and creamy, 15 to 25 minutes. Stir in the nutritional yeast and olive oil, then remove from the heat. Season with salt and pepper to taste. Set aside while you prepare your greens.

5. To make the greens, heat the olive oil in a large skillet over low heat. Add the garlic and sauté until fragrant, about 2 minutes. Add the greens, stir, cover, and cook until wilted. Stir in the lemon juice and cook until the greens are bright green and tender but still have some texture, about 3 minutes.

6. To serve, divide the polenta, tomatoes, and greens among four bowls and top each with about ⅓ cup (80ml) of the crumble.

# Breakfast Tostadas with Refried Black Beans and Cabbage Slaw

SERVES 4

## Refried Beans

1 tablespoon olive oil

1 large white onion, chopped

1 poblano or jalapeño chile, finely chopped

1 clove garlic, minced

3 cups (510g) cooked black beans (see page 101)

½ teaspoon salt

1½ teaspoons chili powder

1 teaspoon ground cumin

½ cup (120ml) vegetable broth, or as needed

2½ tablespoons lime juice

## Cabbage Slaw

3 cups red or green cabbage (or a mixture of both), finely shredded

2 green onions, green parts only, chopped

1½ tablespoons olive oil

1 tablespoon lime juice

2 teaspoons agave nectar

Salt and pepper

8 (6-inch/15cm) corn tortillas

1 large Hass avocado, sliced

½ cup (20g) chopped fresh cilantro

You can make these tostadas as fancy or as simple as you like. If you know you'll be short on time, prepare the refried black beans a day in advance, then throw the cabbage salad together in the morning. If you're preparing them for brunch on a leisurely morning, it's worth your while to make the cashew queso (see right), too. It's the ultimate comfort food sauce—tangy, salty, and versatile. Once you try it, you'll want to smother everything with it, from baked potatoes to steamed broccoli to rice and beans.

1. To make the refried beans, heat the olive oil in a large skillet over medium heat. Add the onion and chile and sauté until the onion is tender and translucent, about 8 minutes. Add the garlic and sauté for 1 minute. Add the black beans, salt, chili powder, and cumin and cook, stirring occasionally, until everything is heated through, adding the vegetable broth as needed to prevent sticking. Remove from the heat and stir in the lime juice. Transfer to a food processor and pulse until fairly smooth, without many whole beans—or to whatever texture you prefer; alternatively, you can use a potato masher or even a fork to mash the beans.

2. Preheat the oven to 325°F (165°C).

3. To make the slaw, put the cabbage, green onions, oil, lime juice, and agave nectar in a bowl and toss until thoroughly combined. Season with salt and pepper to taste.

4. Place the tortillas in a single layer on two baking sheets. Bake for 15 minutes, until crispy. To assemble each tostada, spread about ¼ cup (60ml) of the refried beans on a tortilla. Top with ¼ cup (60ml) of the slaw, a few slices of avocado, and 1 tablespoon of the cilantro.

### For Something Different

**Cashew Queso** In a blender or food processor, puree 1 cup (130g) cashew pieces that have been soaked in water for at least 3 hours and then drained, ⅓ cup (25g) large-flake nutritional yeast, ¾ teaspoon salt, 1 teaspoon chili powder, ½ teaspoon smoked paprika, 1 cup plus 2 tablespoons (265ml) water, 3 tablespoons tomato paste, and 2 tablespoons freshly squeezed lemon juice until totally smooth. Drizzle on top of each tostada before serving.

Appetizers
& Snacks

# Five-Minute No-Bake Granola Bars

SERVES 10 TO 12

2 1/2 cups (225g) rolled oats or quick oats

1 cup (140g) pumpkin seeds

1/2 cup (75g) raisins

2/3 cup (165g) peanut butter or almond butter

1/2 cup (120ml) agave nectar or brown rice syrup, plus more as needed

1/8 teaspoon salt (optional)

This is far and away the most popular recipe I've posted on Food52, and for good reason: it's one of the easiest and most adaptable methods for snack bars ever. Not a fan of peanut butter? Use almond, cashew, or sunflower seed butter. Don't have any pumpkin seeds on hand? Sunflower seeds, cashews, or other nuts will be great, too. As for the dried fruit, anything goes; just be sure to chop larger fruits into small bits.

1. Line an 8 by 8-inch (20 by 20cm) pan with aluminum foil or plastic wrap.

2. In a large bowl, stir together the oats, pumpkin seeds, and raisins.

3. In a medium bowl, stir together the peanut butter, agave nectar, and, if using unsalted peanut butter, the salt; alternatively, combine these ingredients in a food processor and process until well combined. Add to the oat mixture and stir until everything is sticky and well combined. If the mixture is too dry to hold together, add a bit more agave nectar.

4. Spread the mixture in the lined pan, then cover with foil or plastic wrap, and press firmly to form an even layer. Refrigerate for at least 4 hours.

5. Cut into bars and wrap them individually. Stored in the fridge, they'll keep for 2 weeks.

# Baked Kale Chips

SERVES 4

1 large bunch curly kale, stemmed

2 to 3 tablespoons olive oil

Kosher salt and pepper

Kale chips have become such a common snack that you can probably find them at the corner store—but they'll cost you. Making them at home is significantly cheaper and doesn't take much time. There are a few tricks to making a perfectly baked kale chip. One is to coat the kale evenly with oil, so use your hands to massage the olive oil into every last nook and cranny. Another is to spread the kale in an even layer on the baking sheets, without overlapping. Finally, be sure to bake at a low temperature. If the heat is too high, the chips will burn before they take on the crispy texture you're looking for. If you like, sprinkle the chips with smoked paprika, nutritional yeast, chili powder, red pepper flakes, or a combination of seasonings along with the salt and pepper.

1. Preheat the oven to 275°F (135°C).

2. Put the kale in a large bowl, drizzle with the olive oil, then massage the kale until evenly coated. Spread the kale pieces in a single layer on two baking sheets, and season generously with salt and pepper.

3. Bake for 15 minutes, then rotate the pans and bake for about 10 minutes longer, until crispy.

# Crispy Roasted Chickpeas

MAKES ABOUT 2 CUPS (475ML)

2 cups (330g) cooked
chickpeas (see page 101)

2 tablespoons olive oil

1 tablespoon tamari

1 tablespoon freshly
squeezed lemon juice
or balsamic vinegar

Roasted chickpeas are a great, protein-packed snack in their own right, but they also make a wonderful, last-minute addition to soups, salads, grain dishes, stir-fries, and even trail mix. I like them tossed with a handful of raisins for an alternative to salted nuts. Check out the suggested flavor variations, then try your own favorite combinations of spices or seasonings.

1. Preheat the oven to 375°F (190°C). Line a baking sheet with parchment paper or aluminum foil.

2. Put the chickpeas on a clean kitchen towel, fold the towel over them, and pat gently to dry them as well as possible.

3. In a medium bowl, whisk the olive oil, tamari, and lemon juice together. Add the chickpeas and stir gently until evenly coated. Transfer to the lined baking sheet and spread the chickpeas in an even layer.

4. Bake for about 20 minutes, then stir. Bake for 15 minutes longer, until nicely toasted, or 25 minutes longer if you'd like them to be very crunchy.

5. Stored in a sealed container in the refrigerator, the chickpeas will keep for 1 week.

## For Something Different

**Teriyaki-Lime** Toss the chickpeas with a mixture of 2 tablespoons of tamari, 1 clove of garlic (minced), 2 tablespoons of freshly squeezed lime juice, 1 tablespoon of agave nectar, and 1 tablespoon of grated fresh ginger and bake as directed.

**Rosemary-Vinegar** Toss the chickpeas with a mixture of 2 tablespoons of olive oil, 1 tablespoon of apple cider vinegar, 2 tablespoons of chopped fresh rosemary, and 1 teaspoon of coarse sea salt or kosher salt and bake as directed.

**Spicy** Toss the chickpeas with a mixture of 2 tablespoons of olive oil, 1 teaspoon of chili powder, ½ teaspoon of salt, ½ teaspoon of smoked paprika, and a generous pinch of cayenne pepper and bake as directed.

**Brown Sugar** Toss the chickpeas with a mixture of 2 tablespoons of melted coconut oil, 3 tablespoons of brown sugar, 1 teaspoon of ground cinnamon, and a pinch of salt and bake as directed.

# Socca

SERVES 6 TO 8

1 cup (115g) chickpea flour

1 teaspoon salt

Pepper

1½ cups (355ml) water,
at room temperature

3 to 4 tablespoons olive oil

*Socca*, also called *farinata*, is a thin, round gluten-free flatbread made from chickpea flour. It's common in both French and Italian cooking (hence the double name) and requires no yeast or kneading (hooray!). It's usually baked or broiled in a skillet to yield a crispy surface that contrasts with a soft interior. When it's done, you can cut it into wedges and dip it into hummus or olive oil, or even use it as a pizza crust of sorts. My favorite toppings include avocado, salty tapenade, or garlicky sautéed greens. For breakfast or a sweet-savory dessert, you can top it with fresh fruit, compote, or jam.

1. Preheat the oven to 450°F (230°C) and put a 12-inch (30cm) cast-iron skillet in the oven.

2. In a large bowl, whisk together the flour, salt, and pepper in a large bowl. Whisk in 1 cup (240ml) of the water and 2 tablespoons of the olive oil. Let the batter sit for 10 to 15 minutes. If it's very thick, stir in more water as needed to create a thick but pourable batter, similar to pancake batter.

3. Remove the skillet from the oven and coat the pan with 1 tablespoon of the olive oil. Pour the batter into the skillet and bake for 15 minutes, until firm throughout and lightly browning on the edges.

4. For a more a traditional *socca*, turn on the broiler. Brush the top of the socca with the remaining tablespoon of olive oil and broil until browning on top. If you'd like to skip that step, bake it for about 5 minutes longer, until just starting to brown on top.

5. Cut into wedges and serve right away.

# Sesame Flax Crackers

MAKES ABOUT 25 CRACKERS

½ cup (60g) ground flaxseeds

½ cup (80g) golden flaxseeds

½ cup (75g) unhulled sesame seeds

1 cup (240ml) water

1½ tablespoons tamari

½ teaspoon garlic powder

This recipe is super low maintenance: no flour, no rolling pins, and minimal fuss. The nutty taste and binding quality of flaxseeds make them an ideal base for crackers that are crunchy and savory (and healthy!). When the ground flaxseeds soak, they form a gel that binds the rest of the ingredients together; then just spread the mixture on a baking sheet, score it, and pop it in the oven. These crackers are an excellent option for gluten-free guests—and also make an impressive companion to your favorite dip, perhaps Herbed Cashew Cheese (page 136).

1. In a medium bowl, combine all the ingredients and stir well. Cover and let sit at room temperature for 1 hour. The mixture will thicken up considerably and form a dough that is thick and gelatinous but still pourable; add a bit more water if it's too sticky.

2. About 15 minutes before you plan to bake the crackers, preheat the oven to 350°F (175°C). Line a baking sheet with parchment paper.

3. Transfer the dough to the lined baking sheet and spread it as evenly as possible. Score the dough lightly with a pizza roller to indicate the eventual cracker shapes; you can make as few as 15 and as many as 35, but 25 or so is a good number.

4. Bake for 30 to 35 minutes, until lightly browned. Turn off the oven, leave the door slightly ajar, and leave the pan in the oven so the crackers can dry and set.

5. When the crackers are cool, break them apart. Stored in an airtight container at room temperature, the crackers will keep for about 2 weeks.

# Sweet Pea Hummus

SERVES 6

2 cups (330g) cooked chickpeas (see page 101)

1½ cups (210g) fresh or frozen green peas, lightly steamed

3 tablespoons tahini

2 to 3 tablespoons freshly squeezed lemon juice

1 teaspoon chopped garlic

½ teaspoon salt

1 tablespoon olive oil, plus more if needed

1 tablespoon finely grated lemon zest

2 tablespoons chopped fresh herbs, such as dill, parsley, or basil (optional)

Isa Chandra Moskowitz, an esteemed vegan food writer, once said that hummus is a food group for vegans. I agree, but I'd take it a step further and say it's also a food group for students, busy working people, and anyone who likes amazing, healthful food that can be prepared in minutes. The best thing about making your own hummus is that you have total control over the flavors. This version is a light, delicate spin on traditional hummus, featuring fresh green spring peas, lemon zest and juice, and a hint of garlic.

---

1. Put the chickpeas, peas, tahini, lemon juice, garlic, and salt in a food processor or blender (preferably a high-speed blender). Pulse a few times to combine. With the motor running, drizzle in the oil. Keep processing until creamy and smooth, adding a bit more olive oil or water if the hummus is too thick. Add the zest and herbs and pulse to combine.

2. Taste and adjust the seasonings if desired. Stored in a sealed container in the fridge, the hummus will keep for 4 to 5 days.

## How to Get Silky-Smooth Hummus

Most people prefer a smooth consistency to their hummus. If you're one of them, here are a few tricks that will help make your hummus super smooth:

Remove the skins from the cooked chickpeas before blending. It's time-consuming, but it works well.

Warm the chickpeas before blending, either by using just-cooked chickpeas or by heating up canned chickpeas.

If you cook the chickpeas from scratch, use a bit of the cooking liquid in the hummus as you blend; it adds starch, which creates a rich, smooth consistency.

While processing the hummus, stop often to scrape down the sides of the work bowl and incorporate any stray, unblended bits.

# Parsnip Fries with Spicy Harissa Mayonnaise

SERVES 4

**Parsnips**

2½ pounds (1.1kg) parsnips, peeled

2 tablespoons olive oil

Coarse salt and black pepper

**Spicy Harissa Mayonnaise**

1 cup (130g) cashew pieces, soaked in water for at least 3 hours and drained

½ cup (120ml) water

2 tablespoons harissa paste

1 tablespoon freshly squeezed lemon juice

1 teaspoon salt

Pinch of cayenne pepper

This recipe celebrates two often-overlooked ingredients: parsnips, the pale cousins of carrots, and harissa, a smoky and spicy North African chile pepper paste. Once you experience the tender sweetness of parsnip fries, you may be tempted to forsake potatoes. As for the harissa mayonnaise, it's perfectly suited to spicing up most any sandwich or wrap.

---

1. Preheat the oven to 450°F (230°C). Line a baking sheet with parchment paper.

2. To prepare the parsnips, quarter each one lengthwise, then cut in half crosswise. Put the parsnips in a large bowl, drizzle with the olive oil, and toss until evenly coated. Spread them evenly on the lined baking sheet and sprinkle generously with salt and pepper.

3. Bake for 20 to 25 minutes, until the parsnips are turning brown and crispy at the edges, stirring and turning halfway through the baking time.

4. Meanwhile, make the harissa mayonnaise. Put all the ingredients in a food processor or a blender and process until smooth and creamy, stopping occasionally to scrape down the sides of the work bowl. If the mixture is too thick, drizzle in a bit more water while the motor is running.

5. Serve the mayonnaise alongside the parsnip fries. Stored in an airtight container in the fridge, any leftover mayonnaise will keep for 5 days.

# Polenta Squares with Sun-Dried Tomato and Walnut Tapenade

MAKES 24 APPETIZERS

**Polenta**

6 cups (1.4L) vegetable broth, preferably low-sodium

2 cups (250g) fine-grind yellow cornmeal

1 teaspoon salt

1 1/2 teaspoons dried thyme

Pepper

**Tapenade**

2 cups (475ml) boiling water

3/4 cup (40g) sun-dried tomatoes (not oil-packed)

2/3 cup (65g) walnuts

2 small cloves garlic

2 tablespoons freshly squeezed lemon juice

1 tablespoon chopped fresh rosemary

1/2 teaspoon salt

Pepper

1/3 cup (80ml) olive oil

This appetizer feels fancy, but your guests will never know how easy it is to prepare. You can make the polenta and the tapenade 2 days ahead, and then broil and assemble on the day of your party. You can also cut the polenta into thicker slabs and grill it, or even leave it whole to serve as a quick and hearty pizza crust.

1. To make the polenta, pour the broth in a deep saucepan and bring to a boil over medium-high heat. Add the cornmeal in a thin stream, whisking constantly, then add the salt. Adjust the heat to maintain a simmer. Cook, continuing to whisk constantly, until the mixture thickens, then switch to a wooden spoon and cook, stirring constantly, until the polenta is very thick and pulling away from the sides of the pot, about 30 minutes. Stir in the thyme, then season with pepper to taste.

2. Oil a 10 by 15-inch (25 by 38cm) rimmed baking sheet or line it with parchment paper. Spread the polenta evenly over the lined baking sheet with an offset spatula or an inverted knife. Let cool, then cover and refrigerate for a few hours.

3. To make the tapenade, pour the water over the sun-dried tomatoes and let soak for 20 minutes. Drain, retaining 1/2 cup (120ml) of the soaking liquid in case you need to thin the tapenade.

4. Put the walnuts in a food processor and pulse until finely ground. Add the sun-dried tomatoes and garlic and pulse to coarsely chop the tomatoes and combine the ingredients. Add the lemon juice, rosemary, salt, and pepper to taste and pulse briefly. With the motor running, drizzle in the olive oil in a thin stream and process until the mixture has the consistency of a thick pesto. If it's too thick, drizzle in some of the soaking water from the tomatoes while the motor is running.

5. To assemble the appetizers, preheat the broiler. Cut the polenta into 2 1/2-inch (6.5cm) squares by cutting it into quarters lengthwise and sixths crosswise to yield 24 squares. Transfer to a baking sheet and brush lightly with olive oil. Broil for 8 minutes, until lightly toasted. Top each square with a tablespoonful of tapenade and serve.

# Summer Rolls with Spicy Peanut Sauce

MAKES 16 SUMMER ROLLS AND 1½ CUPS (355ML) SAUCE

## Sauce

⅔ cup (160ml) warm water

½ cup (125g) smooth peanut butter

2 tablespoons tamari

2 tablespoons freshly squeezed lime juice

2 teaspoons agave nectar or maple syrup

1 teaspoon toasted sesame oil

1 tablespoon grated fresh ginger, or ½ teaspoon ground

1 clove garlic, crushed

## Rolls

1 cup (20g) loosely packed fresh basil leaves, preferably Thai basil

1 cup (30g) firmly packed fresh cilantro leaves

1 large cucumber, quartered lengthwise, seeded, and julienned

2 cups (240g) julienned jicama

1 cup (70g) finely shredded red cabbage

2 Hass avocados, thinly sliced

16 (8-inch/20cm) rice paper wrappers

Working with rice paper wrappers demands a bit of patience, but the effort is well worth it when you create an appetizer as bright and fresh as this one. And the peanut sauce is so delicious that, once you try a spoonful, you'll want to make an extra batch to keep around for dipping everything in sight.

1. To make the sauce, put all the ingredients in a blender and process until smooth. Alternatively, put them in a medium bowl and whisk until well blended.

2. To prepare the rolls, ready a large clean work surface and have all of the vegetables and herbs lined up in the order listed. Pour about 2 inches (5cm) of warm water into a large, shallow pan. Spread a clean, dry kitchen towel next to the pan. Submerge a rice paper wrapper in the water for about 15 seconds, then lay it on the towel. Flip it over so both sides are dried a bit.

3. Put the rice paper wrapper onto the clean assembly surface. Starting about one-third of the way up from the edge closest to you, spread about 1 tablespoon of the basil across the wrapper, then sprinkle 1 tablespoon of the cilantro atop the basil. Atop the cilantro, make a thin row of the cucumber, then the jicama, then the cabbage, and finally the avocado. Fold the bottom edge of the wrapper up and over the filling. Tuck in the sides of the wrapper, then continue rolling up to the top. Set the roll aside, seam side down, and repeat with the remaining wrappers, herbs, and vegetables.

4. To serve, cut each roll in half at a slight diagonal and offer the sauce alongside.

Soups

# Creamy Tomato Soup

SERVES 4 TO 6

¾ cup (95g) cashew pieces, soaked in water for at least 3 hours and drained

½ cup (120ml) soy milk

½ cup (120ml) vegetable broth

3 tablespoons large-flake nutritional yeast

2 tablespoons olive oil

1 white or yellow onion, coarsely chopped

4 cloves garlic, chopped

2 (14.5-ounce/411g) cans crushed or diced tomatoes, or 1 (28-ounce/794g) can

¼ cup (65g) tomato paste

1 teaspoon dried oregano

½ teaspoon dried thyme

Pinch of red pepper flakes

Salt, to taste

¼ cup (10g) chopped fresh basil

A combination of cashews and soy milk makes this tomato soup smooth, rich, and creamy—just the thing for dunking crusty bread into when you're in need of comfort food. If you like, you can prepare the creamy cashew mixture a day in advance, then store it in the refrigerator until you're ready to make the soup. As a bonus, this soup freezes well, so you can save any leftovers for a rainy afternoon.

1. Put the cashews, soy milk, broth, and nutritional yeast in a blender or food processor and process until completely smooth (which may take a few minutes), stopping occasionally to scrape down the sides of the blender jar.

2. Heat the olive oil in a medium pot over medium heat. Add the onion and sauté until tender and translucent, about 8 minutes. Add the garlic and sauté until very fragrant, 2 or 3 minutes.

3. Stir in the crushed tomatoes, tomato paste, oregano, thyme, pepper flakes, and the blended cashew mixture. Decrease the heat to maintain a simmer. Cook, stirring occasionally, until heated through and thickening slightly.

4. Using an immersion blender (or using a regular blender and working in batches), blend until smooth and creamy, then season with salt to taste. Just before serving, stir in the basil.

### Secret Ingredients for Creamy Soups

There are numerous ways to add creaminess to vegan soups and stews: soy milk and coconut milk, Savory Cashew Cream (page 137), mashed white potatoes, and silken tofu work particularly well.

# Chilled Cucumber Soup with Mango Salsa

SERVES 4

## Soup

2 large cucumbers, peeled and coarsely chopped

1 large Hass avocado

2 green onions, white and green parts, chopped

⅓ cup (80ml) water

2 tablespoons freshly squeezed lime juice

¼ teaspoon salt

¼ teaspoon pepper

## Salsa

1 cup (170g) diced mango, in ½-inch (1.3cm) cubes

½ cup (75g) fresh, raw corn kernels

½ cup (20g) finely chopped fresh cilantro

1 tablespoon olive oil

1 tablespoon freshly squeezed lime juice

Salt and pepper

At the height of summer, chilled soups are a great way to show off fresh produce. And because this soup, which showcases a creamy and sprightly combination of avocado, cucumber, and lime, isn't cooked, it will keep both you and your kitchen cool. The mango and corn salsa adds a touch of sweetness while also providing an interesting textural counterpoint.

1. To make the soup, put all the ingredients in a blender and process until smooth, adding a bit more water if needed to achieve a perfectly creamy texture. Taste and add more salt if desired.

2. To make the salsa, put the mango, corn, cilantro, olive oil, and lime juice in a small bowl and stir until evenly combined. Season to taste with salt and pepper.

3. Serve the soup topped with the salsa.

# Gingered Carrot Bisque

SERVES 4 TO 6

1 tablespoon olive oil

¾ cup (120g) diced onion

½ cup (50g) diced celery

1 (1½-inch/4cm) piece of ginger, finely chopped

4 cups (950ml) vegetable broth

1¼ pounds (680g) carrots, chopped

1 small to medium russet potato, cut into large pieces

1½ teaspoons mild curry powder

Salt

⅓ cup (80ml) Savory Cashew Cream (page 137), plus more for serving

Carrots and ginger play a starring role in this sweet and spicy soup. The supporting cast includes potato for extra heft, cashew cream for a luscious mouthfeel, and a touch of curry powder for deeper, more complex flavor. Just one heads-up: although the cashew cream is super simple to prepare, the cashews must soak for at least 3 hours before making it, so plan ahead.

---

1. Heat the oil in a large pot over medium heat. Add the onion, celery, and ginger and sauté until the onion is tender and translucent, about 8 minutes.

2. Stir in the broth, carrots, potato, and curry powder and bring to a boil. Decrease the heat to maintain a simmer. Cook, stirring occasionally, until the carrots are tender, about 25 minutes.

3. Using an immersion blender (or using a regular blender and working in batches), blend until completely smooth. Put the pot over low heat and cook, stirring often, until heated through. Stir in ⅓ cup of the cashew cream.

4. Top each bowl of bisque with a swirl of cashew cream before serving.

# Corn Chowder with Chive Oil

SERVES 6

**Chowder**

1½ tablespoons olive oil

1 white onion, chopped

2 cloves garlic, minced

1 pound (450g) new potatoes, peeled and diced

½ teaspoon smoked paprika

Kernels from 6 ears of corn (about 3½ cups/540g)

4 cups (950ml) vegetable broth, plus more if needed

¾ teaspoon salt

½ cup (120ml) coconut milk

Pepper

**Chive Oil**

¼ cup (60ml) olive oil

1 ounce (30g) chives, coarsely chopped

Salt

This corn chowder has a touch of sweetness, thanks to the combination of fresh corn and a splash of coconut milk. Potatoes add thickness—a trick you can use to make most any soup creamier. After the soup is cooked, blend it a bit for a chunky soup, or completely for a silky smooth soup. The chive oil has a delicate flavor that adds freshness and balances the sweetness of the corn.

1. To make the chowder, heat the olive oil in a large pot over medium heat. Add the onion and sauté until barely tender, 4 to 5 minutes. Add the garlic and sauté for another minute. Add the potatoes and paprika and cook, stirring constantly, for a couple of minutes.

2. Stir in the corn, broth, and salt and bring to a boil. Decrease the heat to maintain a simmer. Cook, stirring occasionally, until the potatoes are very tender, about 25 minutes, adding a bit more broth if the soup starts to resemble a thick stew. However, don't add too much additional broth, or the final soup will be too thin.

3. Using an immersion blender (or using a regular blender and working in batches), blend the soup until it is about half pureed, with some texture and visible pieces of potato remaining. Stir in the coconut milk, then season with black pepper. Taste and adjust the seasonings if desired.

4. To make the chive oil, put the olive oil and chives in a blender and process until smooth. Season with salt to taste.

5. Serve the chowder with the chive oil drizzled over the top.

# Miso Soup with Shiitakes, Soba, and Asparagus

SERVES 4

6 cups (1.4L) cold water

1 (5-inch/13cm) piece of kombu

1½ to 2 tablespoons minced or grated fresh ginger

1 large or 2 small cloves garlic, finely minced

½ cup (140g) white miso

Tamari (optional)

6 ounces (170g) shiitake mushrooms, stemmed and thinly sliced

4 green onions, green and white parts, chopped

8 ounces (225g) soba

1 pound (450g) asparagus, cut into 2- to 3-inch (5 to 7.5cm) pieces

Optional flavorings and toppings: sriracha sauce, toasted sesame oil, gomasio, or red pepper flakes

This soup begins with making dashi (a basic Japanese sea stock). Traditional dashi uses kombu (a sea vegetable) and dried tuna flakes, but the kombu provides plenty of saltiness and umami all on its own. Then come the miso (you can use almost any variety of miso in this soup, but I prefer white miso because it's a bit less salty and has a mellow, mild flavor), soba noodles, garlic, and ginger that give this soup its spiciness and texture. The asparagus and green onions called for here are great enhancements, but feel free to substitute any quick-cooking vegetables that are in season. You'll want to make this soup year-round; it's light enough for summer, yet warming enough for winter's bleakest days.

1. Put the water and kombu in a large pot and bring to a simmer over medium-high heat. Immediately decrease the heat to maintain a gentle simmer. (Avoid boiling the kombu vigorously, as this can bring out a bitter taste.) Simmer for 10 minutes.

2. Use a slotted spoon to remove the kombu, including any small pieces. Add the ginger and garlic. Ladle a cup or two of the kombu broth into a measuring cup or small bowl, add the miso, and mash with a fork until completely integrated. Stir the miso slurry back into the broth. Taste and adjust the seasoning if you like; you may want to add more ginger or, for a saltier flavor, a splash of tamari. Stir in the shiitakes and green onions.

3. Meanwhile, bring a separate large pot of water to a boil over high heat. Add the soba, decrease the heat to maintain a simmer, and cook, stirring occasionally, until the soba is tender, about 8 minutes.

4. Drain the soba, then add it to the miso broth, along with the asparagus. Simmer until the asparagus is tender, about 5 minutes.

5. Serve immediately, offering any desired optional flavorings and toppings alongside.

# Sweet Potato and Peanut Stew with Kale

SERVES 4

1 tablespoon olive oil

1 yellow onion, diced

2 cloves garlic, crushed

1½ tablespoons minced fresh ginger

2 pounds (900g) sweet potatoes, chopped into 1-inch (2.5cm) chunks

½ cup (95g) red lentils, rinsed well

3 ripe tomatoes, peeled and chopped, or 1 (14.5-ounce/411g) can diced tomatoes

½ teaspoon salt

2 teaspoons ground cumin

1 teaspoon ground cinnamon

½ teaspoon ground turmeric

Cayenne pepper

4 cups (950ml) vegetable broth, plus more as needed

¼ cup (60g) creamy peanut butter

4 cups (300g) finely chopped curly kale

Pepper

¼ cup (25g) chopped green onions, green parts only

¼ cup (35g) roasted, salted peanuts, chopped

This recipe is a cold-weather favorite from my column at Food52. It's been two years since it was published, and readers are still raving about it. Sweet potatoes, red lentils, and tomatoes are simmered with ginger, cumin, and other spices. But what really makes this dish sing is the peanut butter, with its creamy texture and distinctive aroma. And as you're soon to discover, red lentils are a handy thickener for soups and stews; they cook up quickly and become so soft that they sometimes disintegrate into the soup with no pureeing.

1. Heat the olive oil in a large pot over medium heat. Add the onion and sauté until the onion starts to become translucent, about 5 minutes. Add the garlic and ginger and sauté until the garlic is fragrant, about 3 minutes. Add the sweet potatoes, lentils, tomatoes, salt, cumin, cinnamon, turmeric, and a pinch or two of cayenne and stir to combine.

2. Add the vegetable broth. If there isn't enough broth to cover everything by at least 1 inch (2.5cm), add more broth as needed. Stir well and bring to a boil. Decrease the heat to maintain a simmer. Cook, stirring occasionally, until the sweet potatoes and lentils are very tender, 40 to 45 minutes, adding more broth as needed if the stew gets too dry.

3. Add the peanut butter and stir until evenly incorporated. Using an immersion blender (or using a regular blender and working in batches), blend until about half pureed, with some texture remaining. It should be creamy but still have visible chunks of sweet potato.

4. Stir in the kale and cook, stirring occasionally, until the kale is tender. Season with pepper, then taste and adjust the seasonings as desired. Serve topped with the green onions and peanuts.

# Jamaican Jerk Chili with Quinoa and Kidney Beans

SERVES 6

2 tablespoons coconut oil

1 white or yellow onion, chopped

1 green bell pepper, seeded and chopped

1 poblano chile, chopped

2 cloves garlic, minced

1¼ cups (215g) quinoa, rinsed well

1 (28-ounce/794g) can crushed tomatoes, preferably fire-roasted

3 cups (525g) cooked kidney beans (see page 101)

½ teaspoon salt

1 tablespoon chili powder

1 teaspoon ground cinnamon

½ teaspoon dried thyme

½ teaspoon ground nutmeg

¼ teaspoon ground allspice

2½ to 3 cups (590 to 710ml) vegetable broth

1 small Hass avocado (optional), thinly sliced, for garnish

½ cup (20g) chopped fresh cilantro (optional), for garnish

It's a shame quinoa isn't a particularly common chili ingredient, because it adds both texture and heartiness while also freeing you from the monotony of endless bowls of beans. This recipe strays further from tradition by including some spices you might typically think of for baking: cinnamon, nutmeg, and allspice. However, they're all common in Jamaican jerk seasoning—hence this recipe's name—and help bring out the tomatoes' natural sweetness. The resulting dish has all the comfort and heartiness you want from a big bowl of chili, with just enough personality to feel new. (And it smells amazing while it simmers!) This chili freezes nicely, and it pairs well with sautéed kale or slow-cooked collard greens.

---

1. Heat the coconut oil in a large pot over medium heat. Add the onion, bell pepper, and poblano and sauté until the onion is tender and translucent, about 8 minutes. Add the garlic and sauté for 2 minutes longer.

2. Stir in the quinoa, tomatoes, kidney beans, salt, chili powder, cinnamon, thyme, nutmeg, allspice, and 2½ cups (590ml) of the broth and bring to a boil. Decrease the heat to maintain a simmer and cook, stirring occasionally, until the quinoa is plump and tender, with little tails (the germ) emerging from the grains, about 25 minutes. Stir in the remaining ½ cup (120ml) of broth as needed to achieve the desired consistency.

3. Taste and adjust the seasonings as desired. Serve hot, garnished with the avocado and cilantro.

# Smoky Black Bean and Sweet Potato Chili

SERVES 6

1 tablespoon olive oil

2 cups (320g) chopped white or yellow onion

4 cups (540g) diced sweet potatoes, in ¾-inch (2cm) cubes

2 cloves garlic, minced

1 chipotle in adobo, finely chopped (see tip below)

1 tablespoon chili powder

2 teaspoons ground cumin

½ teaspoon smoked paprika

1 (14.5-ounce/411g) can diced tomatoes

3½ cups (600g) cooked black beans (see page 101)

1½ cups (590ml) vegetable broth, plus more as needed

Salt

1 large Hass avocado, sliced, for garnish

¼ cup (10g) thinly sliced chives

This is the chili recipe you want in your back pocket. Sweet potatoes and black beans are a classic pairing, and no recipe shows them off better than this one. This chili is always a hit at potlucks and gatherings. Just be sure to reserve a few servings for your freezer. You'll thank yourself later.

---

1. Heat the oil in a large pot over medium heat. Add the onion and sauté until tender and translucent, about 8 minutes. Then add the sweet potatoes and garlic and sauté until the garlic is fragrant and the sweet potatoes are just becoming tender, 8 to 10 minutes. Add the chipotle in adobo, chili powder, cumin, and paprika and cook, stirring constantly, until the spices are very fragrant. Stir in the tomatoes, beans, and broth and bring to a boil. Decrease the heat to maintain a simmer. Cook, stirring occasionally, until the sweet potatoes are tender, 30 to 35 minutes, adding more broth as needed to achieve the desired consistency. Season with salt to taste.

2. Let the chili sit for a few minutes so the flavors meld. Serve topped with the avocado and chives.

### How to Add Smoky Flavor to Vegan Dishes

I have two favorite methods for creating smoky flavor in vegan recipes. One is to use a bit of smoked paprika. Both sweet and hot paprika can be found in smoked forms; any online spice merchant should sell them, and smoked paprika can often be found at grocery stores with a good spice selection. The other is to use chipotle chiles in adobo sauce, a rich blend of paprika, oregano, garlic, salt, and vinegar. Both are used in this recipe to create an especially smoky flavor.

Salads

# Greek Salad with Tofu Feta

SERVES 4 TO 6

**Salad**

1 large cucumber, halved lengthwise, seeded, and chopped into ¾- to 1-inch (2 to 2.5cm) pieces

2 heaping cups (375g) seeded and diced tomatoes, in 1-inch (2.5cm) pieces (3 to 4 tomatoes)

¾ cup (100g) pitted kalamata olives, halved

½ cup (60g) thinly sliced red onion

⅓ cup (15g) chopped fresh Italian parsley

**Vinaigrette**

¼ cup (60ml) olive oil

2 tablespoons red wine vinegar

1 tablespoon freshly squeezed lemon juice

1 teaspoon dried oregano

¼ teaspoon salt

Pepper

14 ounces (400g) Tofu Feta (page 136)

2 pita breads (optional), cut into wedges, for serving

This recipe offers all the flavors of a traditional Greek salad—including the cheese, thanks to Tofu Feta. Just be aware that the tofu cheese must marinate for at least 4 hours. The good news: you can prepare it up to 2 days in advance of using it, and once that's done, putting the salad together is a breeze. The red wine vinaigrette is a handy, all-purpose dressing that can be used on all sorts of salads and on steamed vegetables.

---

1. To make the salad, put all the ingredients in a large bowl and toss to combine.

2. To make the vinaigrette, put the olive oil, vinegar, lemon juice, oregano, and salt in a small bowl or measuring cup and whisk until well blended. Season with pepper.

3. Drizzle the dressing over the salad and stir gently until all the ingredients are evenly coated. Add the tofu feta and toss gently to combine. Serve with the pita wedges alongside.

# Kale Salad with Kabocha Squash, Toasted Hazelnuts, and Pomegranate Seeds

SERVES 4

1 small kabocha squash (about 1 pound/450g), cut into 1.5-inch (4cm) pieces

4 tablespoons (60ml) olive oil

Salt and pepper

½ cup (65g) hazelnuts

2 tablespoons freshly squeezed lemon juice

1 teaspoon Dijon mustard

1 teaspoon maple syrup

1 large bunch curly kale, stemmed and torn into bite-size pieces

¾ cup (130g) pomegranate seeds

Kale salads are so popular these days that it's easy to take them for granted. But a great one can still be showstopping, as is the case here, in part thanks to the lively vinaigrette and tart, crimson pomegranate seeds. The creamy and colorful kabocha squash gives substance to the dish, so you can serve it as a filling appetizer or a lighter meal. This is an ideal salad for holiday entertaining, or just for brightening your table on a chilly winter night.

---

1. Preheat the oven to 375°F (190°C).

2. Toss the squash with 1 tablespoon of the olive oil, then spread on a rimmed baking sheet. Sprinkle with salt and pepper. Bake for 15 minutes, then stir well. Bake for 15 to 20 minutes longer, until tender. Let cool to room temperature.

3. Meanwhile, spread the hazelnuts in a small baking pan or pie plate and toast in the oven for 4 to 6 minutes, until golden. Check them frequently and remove them the moment they start to get brown. Let cool slightly, then rub the nuts between paper towels to help remove the skins. Coarsely chop the nuts.

4. Put the remaining 3 tablespoons of olive oil in a small bowl or cup. Add the lemon juice, mustard, maple syrup, and ¼ teaspoon of salt and whisk until well blended. Season with pepper.

5. Put the kale in a large bowl and drizzle with 3 tablespoons of the dressing. Massage the dressing into the kale with your hands until the kale has a soft, almost wilted texture. Add the squash, hazelnuts, and pomegranate seeds and toss gently until all the ingredients are evenly coated. Taste and mix in more dressing if desired.

6. Divide the salad among four plates and serve. Stored in a covered container in the fridge, any leftovers will keep for 1 day.

# Heirloom Tomato and Golden Beet Panzanella

SERVES 4

6 tablespoons (90ml) olive oil

2 heaping tablespoons capers, patted dry with a paper towel

1 small whole wheat sourdough boule, cut into 1-inch (2.5cm) cubes (5 to 6 cups/1.2 to 1.4L)

12 ounces (340g) golden beets, peeled and cut into 1-inch (2.5cm) cubes (4 medium or 3 large beets)

Salt

4 heirloom tomatoes, cut into 1-inch (2.5cm) chunks

Pepper

¼ cup (10g) thinly sliced fresh basil

I love the way crisp, toasted sourdough bread contrasts with tender beets and juicy tomatoes in this late-summer panzanella salad. Yellow beets add a nice color, and they're also a little sweeter than red beets, especially when roasted. That said, any beets—red, yellow, chioggia (striped)—will do.

1. Preheat the oven to 350°F (175°C).

2. Heat 3 tablespoons of the olive oil in a small skillet over medium-high heat. Add the capers and cook, stirring occasionally, until very crispy but not burnt, about 2 minutes. Remove the capers from the heat and set aside.

3. Spread the bread cubes evenly on two rimmed baking sheets and bake for 20 to 25 minutes, until brown and crispy, stirring halfway through.

4. Increase the oven temperature to 400°F (200°C) and line a baking sheet with parchment paper.

5. Toss the beets with about 2 tablespoons of the olive oil, then arrange the cubes on the lined baking sheet. Sprinkle with a bit of salt. Bake for 25 to 35 minutes, until tender and just browning at the edges. Let cool to room temperature.

6. Put the tomatoes and beets in a large bowl. Drizzle with the remaining tablespoon of olive oil and season with salt and pepper. Add the capers, bread cubes, and basil and gently toss until evenly combined. Taste and adjust the seasonings if desired. Serve cold or at room temperature. Stored in a covered container in the fridge, any leftovers will keep for 1 day.

# Snow Pea, Cabbage, and Mizuna Salad with Smoky Tempeh

SERVES 4, MAKES 1½ CUPS (355ML) DRESSING

**Salad**

6 ounces (170g) snow peas, trimmed

2 cups (140g) shredded red cabbage

2 cups (60g) mizuna

1 cup (110g) shredded carrots

2 green onions, white and green parts, thinly sliced

¼ cup (10g) coarsely chopped fresh cilantro

**Dressing**

⅔ cup (160ml) water, plus more if desired

½ cup (125g) tahini

2 tablespoons toasted sesame oil

2 tablespoons tamari

2 tablespoons rice vinegar

1 tablespoon maple syrup

1 clove garlic, minced

1 teaspoon minced fresh ginger

8 ounces (225g) Smoky Tempeh (page 94)

This dish is all about contrast: Subtly spicy mizuna meets sweet, crispy snow peas, with earthy, salty tempeh layered atop both. Then there's the extremely versatile sesame tahini dressing, which has a salty, sweet flavor that also shines in simple brown rice bowls and salads and as a dip for raw vegetables.

1. To make the salad, bring a small pot of water to a boil and blanch the snow peas for about 30 seconds. Rinse under cold water to stop the cooking. Drain well and let dry, or pat with a clean kitchen towel to dry them more quickly. Cut the snow peas in halves or thirds.

2. Put the snow peas in a large bowl. Add the cabbage, mizuna, carrots, green onions, and cilantro and toss to combine.

3. To make the dressing, combine all the ingredients in a blender and process until smooth. Add a bit more water to thin the dressing if you like. Be aware that it will thicken when chilled.

4. Drizzle ⅔ cup (160ml) of all the dressing over the salad and toss until all the ingredients are evenly coated. Add more dressing to taste. Serve topped with the tempeh.

## Building a Meal-Worthy Salad

Only when I became vegan did I begin to understand the remarkable diversity of salads. Now meal-size salads are one of my favorite casual dinners. Mine typically include a cooked whole grain, a variety of vegetables, and a mixture of legumes, nuts, and seeds, all enhanced with a bold dressing. As you explore the recipes in this chapter, think about how you can add heft and substance to your salads with different combinations of grains, dried fruit, nuts, seeds, legumes, proteins, and greens.

# French Lentil and Arugula Salad with Herbed Cashew Cheese

SERVES 4

1/3 cup (80ml) olive oil

1 small shallot, minced

1 teaspoon salt

2 tablespoons freshly squeezed lemon juice

1 tablespoon champagne vinegar

1 teaspoon Dijon mustard

2 1/2 cups (375g) cooked Le Puy green lentils (see below), drained well

2 cups (60g) firmly packed baby arugula leaves

1 cup (115g) thinly sliced radishes

1 cup (50g) chopped endive

1 cup (105g) sliced cucumber

1/4 cup (12g) chopped fresh dill

1/3 cup (35g) toasted walnuts, chopped

Pepper

1/4 cup (60ml) Herbed Cashew Cheese (page 136)

This salad is inspired by that traditional combination of Le Puy lentils, walnuts, and goat cheese, with crisp arugula and radishes adding a welcome crunch and a peppery kick. In place of the goat cheese, I use tangy, salty Herbed Cashew Cheese (page 136). Making the cashew cheese requires some forethought, so if you don't have any on hand or time to make it, you can omit it or substitute a chopped avocado.

---

1. In a small bowl or measuring cup, whisk together the olive oil, shallot, salt, lemon juice, vinegar, and mustard until evenly blended.

2. In a large bowl, stir together the lentils, arugula, radishes, endive, cucumber, and dill. Drizzle evenly with the dressing, then toss or stir until all the ingredients are evenly coated. Stir in the walnuts and season with black pepper to taste. Dot the top of the salad with small bits of the cashew cheese (about 1/2 teaspoon each).

3. Serve the salad right away, or store in an airtight container in the fridge for up to 3 days.

## The Best Way to Cook Lentils

Good news: lentils are quicker to prepare from scratch than beans and add great texture and nutrition to dishes. To cook them, start with about 1 cup (200g) of red, brown, or Le Puy (green) lentils. Pick out any that are discolored or shriveled. Rinse the lentils under running water, then combine them in a saucepan with 2 1/2 cups (590ml) of water. Bring the water to a rapid simmer, then reduce to a gentle simmer. Add extra water as needed so that the lentils remain barely submerged. Simmer the lentils for 20 to 30 minutes, until they're tender but retain some chew. (Red lentils take less time to cook because they've been split, so they'll likely be tender in 20 to 25 minutes.) Drain them, then season with salt and pepper to taste. 1 cup (200g) of dry red, brown, or Le Puy lentils will make between 2 and 2 1/4 cups (400 to 450g) of cooked lentils.

# Roasted Cauliflower and Freekeh Salad

SERVES 4

1 pound (450g) cauliflower, cut into bite-size pieces

6 tablespoons (80ml) olive oil

Salt and pepper

1½ cups (355ml) vegetable broth

¾ cup (170g) freekeh

2 tablespoons freshly squeezed lemon juice

1 teaspoon Dijon mustard

½ cup (75g) dried currants or raisins

1 tablespoon finely grated lemon zest

3 tablespoons finely chopped fresh mint

Freekeh is another name for green wheat kernels that have been cracked and toasted. It has a distinctively nutty taste and is a great alternative to couscous or quinoa in grain-based salads. This recipe marries freekeh with crispy roasted cauliflower and accents the satisfying combination with lemon, freshly chopped mint, and other bright seasonings. Like most grain salads, this recipe keeps well, so you can serve it for guests one night and enjoy leftovers for lunch the next day. If you can't find freekeh, bulgur wheat is a fine substitute; use ¼ cup (55g) of bulgur and cook it as you would quinoa (see page 93), extending the cooking time to 20 to 25 minutes.

---

1. Preheat the oven to 425°F (220°C).

2. Toss the cauliflower florets with 2 tablespoons of the olive oil. Spread the cauliflower evenly on a rimmed baking sheet and sprinkle with salt and pepper. Bake for 20 minutes, until browning and getting crispy. Let cool to room temperature.

3. Meanwhile, combine the broth and freekeh in a medium saucepan and bring to a boil over medium-high heat. Decrease the heat to maintain a simmer, cover, and cook for 20 minutes, until the freekeh is tender and has absorbed all the broth. Fluff the freekeh with a fork, then let it cool a bit.

4. Put the remaining 4 tablespoons (60ml) olive oil in a small bowl or measuring cup. Add the lemon juice, mustard, ½ teaspoon of pepper, and ¼ teaspoon of salt and whisk until well blended.

5. In a large bowl, gently stir together the cauliflower, freekeh, currants, and lemon zest. Drizzle with the dressing and toss until all the ingredients are evenly coated. Taste and adjust the seasonings if desired. Just before serving, stir in the mint.

6. Serve cold or at room temperature. Stored in a covered container in the fridge, any leftovers will keep for 3 days.

# Quinoa Salad with Sweet Potatoes, Kale, and Pesto Vinaigrette

SERVES 4; MAKES 1½ CUPS (355ML) VINAIGRETTE

**Salad**

2 medium sweet potatoes, peeled and diced into ½-inch (1.3cm) pieces

2 tablespoons olive oil

Salt and pepper

1 cup (170g) quinoa

2 cups (475ml) vegetable broth

2 cups (150g) stemmed and finely chopped curly kale

½ cup (70g) roasted, salted sunflower seeds

⅓ cup (13g) thinly sliced fresh basil

**Vinaigrette**

½ cup (15g) firmly packed fresh basil leaves

¼ cup (8g) firmly packed fresh parsley leaves

½ cup (120ml) olive oil

¼ cup (60ml) freshly squeezed lemon juice

1 clove garlic, minced

1 teaspoon agave nectar or maple syrup

¼ teaspoon salt

Pepper

This is a salad for August or September, when basil still abounds at the farmers' market and sweet potatoes are just coming into season. It's full of texture—crispy kale, crunchy sunflower seeds, and soft, roasted sweet potatoes—and it definitely qualifies as meal-worthy. The pesto vinaigrette is one of my all-time favorites. (As a bonus, it freezes well.) You can vary the herbs in the vinaigrette based on what's in season—mint, tarragon, and thyme make nice additions. All renditions of this dressing are fabulous over roasted vegetables or whole grains.

---

1. Preheat the oven to 425°F (220°C).

2. To make the salad, toss the sweet potatoes with the olive oil, then spread them evenly on a rimmed baking sheet. Sprinkle with salt and pepper. Bake for 10 minutes, then stir well. Bake for 10 to 15 minutes longer, until tender and browning. Let cool to room temperature.

3. Meanwhile, put the quinoa in a fine-mesh sieve and rinse until the water runs clear (see page 93). Put the quinoa and broth in a medium saucepan and bring to a boil over medium-high heat. Decrease the heat to maintain a simmer, cover, and cook for 20 minutes, until the quinoa has absorbed all the liquid. Fluff the quinoa with a fork and let cool to room temperature.

4. Meanwhile, make the vinaigrette. Combine all the ingredients in a blender or food processor and process until mostly smooth but with small pieces of herbs still visible.

5. In a large bowl, gently stir together the sweet potatoes, quinoa, kale, sunflower seeds, and basil. Drizzle with about ⅓ cup (80ml) of the dressing and gently stir until all of the ingredients are evenly coated. Taste and mix in more dressing if desired.

6. Serve cold or at room temperature. Stored in a covered container in the fridge, any leftovers will keep for 2 days.

# Wheat Berry and Green Bean Salad with Dried Cranberries and Celery

SERVES 4

1 cup (180g) wheat berries, soaked in water for at least 8 hours and drained

1½ cups (150g) green beans, cut into 1½-inch (4cm) pieces

1 cup (100g) thinly sliced celery

1 green onion, white and green parts, chopped

¼ cup (10g) chopped parsley

⅓ cup (40g) dried cranberries

½ cup (60g) coarsely chopped toasted pecans

3 tablespoons olive oil, walnut oil, or hazelnut oil

2 tablespoons freshly squeezed lemon juice

Salt and pepper

This is the ultimate salad for Thanksgiving or any winter get-together. It combines a number of well-loved holiday ingredients in a slightly untraditional way, highlighting crispy celery, flavorful pecans, crunchy green beans, sweet cranberries, and zesty green onions. The wheat berries make it hearty enough that it can even serve as a main dish when other vegan options are scarce.

1. Put the wheat berries in a medium saucepan and add enough water to cover them by a few inches. Bring to a boil over medium-high heat. Decrease the heat to maintain a simmer, cover, and cook for 35 minutes, until tender (taste a few to make sure they're uniformly cooked through). Drain well, then transfer to a large bowl and let cool to room temperature.

2. Fill a bowl with ice-cold water. Bring a medium pot of water to a boil. Add the green beans and cook just until crisp-tender, about 2 minutes. Quickly drain the beans and plunge them into the bowl of cold water to stop the cooking. Drain well.

3. Add the beans, celery, green onion, parsley, cranberries, and pecans to the wheat berries and stir gently until well combined. In a small bowl or measuring cup, whisk together the olive oil and lemon juice until well blended. Drizzle over the salad and stir gently until everything is evenly coated. Season with salt and pepper to taste. Serve cold or at room temperature. Stored in a covered container in the fridge, the salad will keep for 2 days.

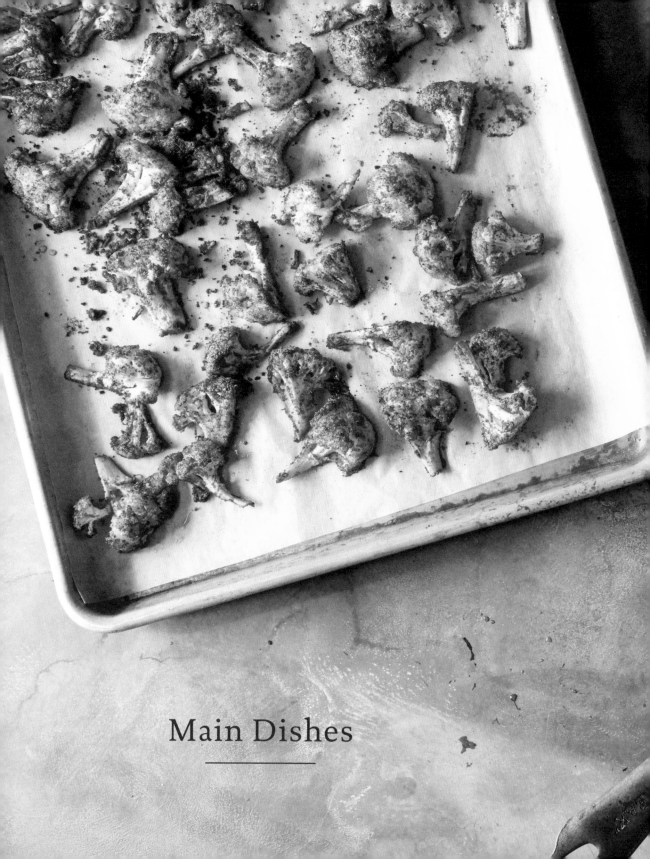

# Main Dishes

# Penne with Summer Squash, Corn, and Herbs

SERVES 4

4 cups (540g) cherry
tomatoes

2 large zucchini or summer
squash, halved lengthwise,
then sliced crosswise ½ inch
(1.3cm) thick

1 large red onion, chopped

2 cloves garlic, crushed

4 tablespoons (60ml)
olive oil

Coarse salt and pepper

Kernels from 2 ears of corn
(about 1¼ cups/180g)

8 ounces (225g) penne
or farfalle pasta

⅓ cup (7g) torn fresh basil
leaves

1 tablespoon chopped fresh
oregano

¼ cup (35g) toasted pine
nuts (optional)

This is summer in a bowl, with sweet corn, slouchy cherry tomatoes, and tender zucchini lightening up a savory, satisfying bowl of pasta. It's just the kind of recipe to turn to when you have friends coming over on a hot night and you don't want to spend much time at the stove.

1. Preheat the oven to 450°F (230°C).

2. In a large bowl, gently stir together the tomatoes, zucchini, onion, and garlic. Drizzle with 3 tablespoons of the olive oil and season generously with salt and pepper. Stir gently until the vegetables are evenly coated. Transfer to two rimmed baking sheets and spread in an even layer.

3. Bake for 20 to 25 minutes. Stir in the corn and bake for about 15 minutes, until the vegetables are sweet and golden brown; in order for the vegetables to caramelize in this way, stir them minimally while baking.

4. Meanwhile, bring a large pot of salted water to a boil over high heat. Stir in the pasta, then adjust the heat to maintain a low boil. Cook, stirring occasionally, until the pasta is tender but slightly al dente. Drain, reserving a small amount of the cooking liquid. Return the pasta to the pot.

5. Add the vegetables, along with the remaining 1 tablespoon of olive oil and a bit of the cooking liquid, and stir gently to combine. Gently stir in the basil and oregano. Serve topped with the pine nuts.

## Choosing Pasta

Most fresh pastas do contain egg, so I recommend using any of the popular dry brands (like Barilla or De Cecco), or your favorite artisanal vegan brand. Brown rice and quinoa pastas are also both vegan-friendly.

# Orecchiette with Creamy Leeks and Broccoli Rabe

SERVES 4

## Sauce

1 tablespoon olive oil

2 large shallots, chopped

2 cloves garlic, minced

8 ounces (225g) silken tofu

3 tablespoons large-flake nutritional yeast

½ teaspoon salt

Pinch of ground nutmeg

1 teaspoon freshly squeezed lemon juice

¼ cup (60ml) water, or as needed

Pepper

## Pasta and Vegetables

8 ounces (225g) orecchiette

2 tablespoons olive oil

2 large leeks, chopped and thoroughly rinsed

2 bunches broccoli rabe, stemmed and coarsely chopped

1 clove garlic, minced

1 tablespoon freshly squeezed lemon juice

2 tablespoons chopped fresh chives

The luscious sauce in this dish is reminiscent of Alfredo, but because it relies on silken tofu for creaminess, it feels lighter and fresher. It contrasts beautifully with the bitter, almost spicy broccoli rabe and soft, sweet leeks. This dish is elegant enough to serve to guests but simple enough to whip up on a weeknight. Feel free to vary the vegetables according to the season. In springtime, tender green peas are a really lovely addition.

---

1. To make the sauce, heat the olive oil in a medium skillet over medium heat. Add the shallots and sauté until fragrant and tender, about 3 minutes. Add the garlic and sauté for another minute or two.

2. Transfer the contents of the skillet to a blender or food processor. Add the tofu, nutritional yeast, salt, nutmeg, and lemon juice and process until thick and creamy, drizzling in the water as needed to achieve the desired consistency. Season with pepper to taste.

3. To prepare the pasta and vegetables, bring a large pot of salted water to a boil over high heat. Stir in the pasta, then adjust the heat to maintain a low boil. Cook, stirring occasionally, until the pasta is tender but slightly al dente. Drain well.

4. Meanwhile, heat the olive oil in a large skillet over medium heat. Add the leeks and sauté until lightly golden. Add the broccoli rabe and sauté until just tender, 2 to 3 minutes. Add the garlic and lemon juice and sauté until the garlic is lightly golden, about 2 minutes.

5. Put the pasta in a large bowl. Add the leek mixture and about ½ cup (120ml) of the sauce and stir gently to combine. The dish should be quite creamy but not drowning in sauce, so gently stir in more sauce as needed. Serve topped with the chives.

# Butternut Squash Mac and Cheese

SERVES 6 TO 8

1½ to 2 pounds (680 to 900g) butternut squash (about 1 medium squash), peeled and cubed

2 tablespoons olive oil

Salt and pepper

3 cloves garlic, coarsely chopped

½ cup (120ml) coconut milk

1¼ cups (300ml) unsweetened almond milk, homemade (page 134) or store-bought

½ cup plus 2 tablespoons (45g) large-flake nutritional yeast

1 tablespoon arrowroot powder

¼ teaspoon smoked paprika

2 tablespoons freshly squeezed lemon juice

1 tablespoon white miso

1 pound (450g) elbow pasta

2 cups (about 475ml) cooked vegetables (optional), such as steamed chopped spinach, blanched peas, or lightly steamed broccoli florets

½ cup (55g) dry breadcrumbs

Everyone has a favorite mac and cheese recipe. This one, which uses sweet, creamy butternut squash in the sauce, is mine. To create an authentic cheese flavor, I use a combination of nutritional yeast, miso, smoked paprika, salt, and lemon juice. (You can even use any leftover sauce as a cheese dip.) I highly recommend including the optional vegetables. In addition to providing some contrasting color and texture, they'll round out the meal, so you won't have to worry about making an extra side dish—win, win.

1. Preheat the oven to 400°F (230°C). Oil a 7 by 11-inch (18 by 28cm) pan.

2. Coat the squash with 1 tablespoon of the olive oil, then spread it evenly on a rimmed baking sheet. Sprinkle with salt and pepper.

3. Bake for 30 to 35 minutes, until very tender and just starting to brown. Remove from the oven. Decrease the oven temperature to 350°F (175°C).

4. Meanwhile, heat the remaining tablespoon of olive oil in a small saucepan over medium-low heat. Add the garlic and sauté for 2 to 3 minutes, until just starting to brown. Add the coconut milk and ¾ cup (175ml) of the almond milk. Whisk in the nutritional yeast and arrowroot powder. Cook, whisking constantly, until nice and thick, about 5 minutes. Transfer the sauce to a large bowl and add the remaining ½ cup (120ml) of almond milk, the butternut squash, 1 teaspoon of salt, ¼ teaspoon of pepper, and the paprika, lemon juice, and miso. Stir to distribute the ingredients somewhat evenly. Working in batches, transfer to a blender or food processor and process until totally smooth and creamy.

5. Bring a pot of salted water to boil over high heat. Add a drizzle of olive oil to prevent sticking. Stir in the pasta and adjust the heat to maintain a low boil. Cook, stirring occasionally, until the pasta is al dente. Drain well and let cool briefly.

6. Put the pasta in a large bowl and add the vegetables. Add the sauce, using only 2 cups (475ml) of it if not adding the optional vegetables. Stir gently until thoroughly combined. Spread the mixture evenly in the prepared pan and scatter the breadcrumbs evenly over the top.

7. Bake for 20 minutes, until the top is golden. Serve right away.

# Asparagus, Arugula, and Pesto Pizza

SERVES 4

## Pizza Dough

1 cup (240ml) lukewarm water (no hotter than 110°F/43°C)

2 ½ teaspoons active dry yeast

1 tablespoon sugar

2 ½ cups (315g) unbleached bread flour

1 teaspoon salt

1 tablespoon olive oil

## Pesto

2 cups (60g) firmly packed fresh basil leaves

½ cup walnuts (50g) or pine nuts (70g)

1 to 2 cloves garlic, coarsely chopped

½ cup (120ml) olive oil

3 tablespoons large-flake nutritional yeast

1 tablespoon freshly squeezed lemon juice

Salt and pepper

## Toppings

12 ounces (340g) asparagus, halved crosswise

2 cups (40g) loosely packed baby arugula leaves

This pizza is a celebration of spring. Bursting with the flavors of zesty arugula, lemony basil, and grassy asparagus, it's as fresh and light as can be. That said, the basic recipe is very versatile, so change it up with the seasons, topping it with tomatoes and peppers in summer, butternut squash and sage in autumn, caramelized onions and cauliflower in winter—you get the idea. The pesto recipe here is a keeper, with a distinctively cheesy flavor thanks to the nutritional yeast. Once you've tasted it, you'll want to keep it on hand for pasta and sandwiches, to top veggies or cooked grains, or even just to spread on a cracker. Stored in the fridge, it will keep for 5 days.

---

1. To make the dough, put the water in a small bowl. Add the yeast and sugar and stir to dissolve. Let stand for 5 to 10 minutes, until a thin layer of bubbles covers the surface of the water.

2. In a large bowl, whisk together the flour and salt. Make a well in the center and pour in the yeast mixture and oil. Stir with a wooden spoon until the dough gets too sticky to handle, then mix with your hands until uniform.

3. Transfer the dough to a lightly floured work surface and knead for 10 minutes, until elastic and smooth.

4. Shape the dough into a ball and put it in a well-oiled bowl. Cover with plastic wrap or a kitchen towel and let rise at room temperature until doubled in size, about 3 hours. At this point, you can gently deflate the dough and divide it into two pieces, flatten each into a thick disk, and refrigerate them, wrapped in plastic, for up to 36 hours. Allow them to come back to room temperature before shaping into crust and baking.

5. If you're proceeding to make the pizza, preheat the oven to 450°F (230°C). Dust two baking sheets with cornmeal or flour.

6. To make the pesto, put the basil, walnuts, and garlic in a food processor and pulse until the ingredients are coarsely ground. With the motor running, drizzle in the olive oil. Scrape down the sides, then add the yeast and lemon juice and pulse to combine. Season with salt and pepper to taste.

7. To assemble and bake the pizzas, put the two pieces of dough on a lightly floured work surface. Roll out the dough to form a circle with a diameter of 10 to 12 inches (25 to 30cm). Carefully transfer each to one of the dusted baking sheets. Spread half of the pesto over each. Distribute the asparagus evenly over the pizzas.

8. Bake for 20 to 22 minutes, until the crust is golden and the asparagus is lightly browned. Sprinkle half of the arugula over each pizza. Cut each pizza into halves or thirds and serve right away.

# Carrot and Fennel Pot Pie

SERVES 6

## Crust

1 3/4 cups (220g) unbleached all-purpose flour

1/2 teaspoon salt

1/2 cup (110g) coconut oil, cold or at cool room temperature

1/4 cup (60ml) ice water, plus more as needed

## Filling

1 tablespoon olive oil

1 yellow onion, chopped

3 stalks celery, diced

2 carrots, peeled and diced

1 cup (105g) coarsely chopped fennel

2 cloves garlic, minced

2 cups (475ml) vegetable broth

1 russet potato, peeled and diced

3 tablespoons unbleached all-purpose flour

Salt and pepper

1 cup (140g) frozen green peas

1/4 cup (10g) chopped parsley

This pot pie has all of the buttery flavor and richness of traditional versions, complete with a flaky crust thanks to the amazing powers of coconut oil. Carrots and fennel provide subtle sweetness in the filling and play nicely with the slightly peppery parsley; however, feel free to use any fresh or dried herbs you like. Leftovers? Not a problem. This pot pie just gets tastier after a day or two. Plus, the crust can be made in advance; unbaked and wrapped well, it will keep for 4 days in the fridge or 1 month in the freezer.

---

1. To make the crust, put the flour and salt in a food processor and pulse briefly to combine. Add the coconut oil and pulse until the mixture resembles a coarse meal. With the motor running, slowly drizzle in the ice water, using just enough to bring the dough together. Shape the dough into a disk, then wrap it in plastic wrap and put it in the fridge.

2. To make the filling, heat the olive oil in a large pot over medium heat. Add the onion, celery, and carrots and sauté until the onion is tender and translucent, about 8 minutes. Add the fennel and garlic and sauté until all the vegetables are tender, about 6 minutes. Stir in the broth and potato and bring to a boil. Decrease the heat to maintain a simmer and cook, stirring occasionally, until the potato is tender, about 10 minutes.

3. Sprinkle in the flour and stir until evenly incorporated. Cook, stirring often, until considerably thickened, about 5 minutes. Season with salt and pepper to taste. Remove from the heat and stir in the peas and parsley.

4. Preheat the oven to 400°F (200°C).

5. To assemble and bake the pot pie, transfer the filling to an 8-inch (20cm) square baking pan or a pie tin of a similar size. Roll out the dough until just a bit larger than the baking pan; it should be about 1/8 inch (3mm) thick. Carefully transfer the dough to the pan, setting it directly atop the filling, and trim away any excess. Cut a few small slits in the top to allow steam to escape during baking.

6. Bake for 30 to 40 minutes, until the filling is bubbly and the top is golden. Let cool for at least 15 minutes before serving.

# Mushroom, Pecan, and Lentil Burgers

MAKES 4 TO 6 PATTIES

2 tablespoons olive oil

1½ cups (240g) chopped onion

4 cups (280g) chopped cremini mushrooms

2 cloves garlic, minced

1 tablespoon chopped fresh thyme, or 2 teaspoons dried

2 teaspoons chopped fresh oregano, or 1 teaspoon dried

½ cup (60g) toasted pecans, chopped

1 cup (200g) cooked red lentils (see page 71)

2 tablespoons tamari

1 tablespoon white miso

1½ cups (165g) breadcrumbs, preferably whole grain

Pepper

Mushrooms are rich in umami, that fifth flavor that a lot of people describe as "savoriness," so they're a big part of what makes these burgers taste so rich and satisfying. Some veggie burgers highlight the flavors of vegetables; others manage to replicate an authentically meaty flavor. These are the latter. I serve them with ketchup, a squeeze of Spicy Harissa Mayonnaise (page 37), and a few slices of avocado.

---

1. If you'd like to bake the burgers rather than fry them, preheat the oven to 350°F (175°C). Line a baking sheet with parchment paper.

2. Heat the olive oil in a large skillet over medium heat. Add the onion and sauté until browning slightly, about 8 minutes. Add the mushrooms, garlic, thyme, and oregano and sauté until the mushrooms are cooked through, about 5 minutes. Remove from the heat.

3. Put the pecans in a food processor and pulse until finely ground. Add the mushroom mixture, lentils, tamari, and miso. Pulse until well combined and uniform, but with some texture remaining.

4. Transfer to a large bowl. Add the breadcrumbs and mix them in by hand. Season with pepper, then taste and adjust the seasonings if desired. Shape the mixture into 4 large patties or 6 smaller ones.

5. Bake the burgers on the lined baking sheet for 15 minutes, then flip and bake for 15 minutes longer, until brown. Alternatively, heat a couple teaspoons of olive oil in a skillet over medium-high heat and fry the burgers until crisp on both sides. Serve hot, with toppings of choice. Stored in a covered container, the burgers will keep for 4 days in the fridge.

## Building a Better Veggie Burger

Vegetable burgers can be tricky. If the amount of liquid or beans is too great, they'll be dense and gummy; if the amount of grains or breadcrumbs is too great, they may be dry. I find that using equal quantities of cooked legumes or ground nuts or seeds, on the one hand, and cooked whole grains or breadcrumbs, on the other, is best for a reliable consistency.

# Zucchini Quinoa Cakes

MAKES 6 PATTIES

1 tablespoon olive oil

1 cup (160g) finely chopped onion

1 clove garlic, minced

1½ cups (255g) julienned or coarsely grated zucchini

Salt and pepper

½ cup (70g) raw or toasted pumpkin seeds

1½ cups (250g) cooked chickpeas (see page 101)

1 cup (185g) cooked quinoa (see page 93)

2 tablespoons chopped fresh dill

1 tablespoon chopped fresh oregano

1 teaspoon paprika

2 tablespoons Dijon mustard

1 tablespoon freshly squeezed lemon juice

Water as needed

These quinoa cakes are reminiscent of veggie burgers, but they're lighter than the Mushroom, Pecan, and Lentil Burgers (page 90). The combination of quinoa, which is less dense than other grains, and moist zucchini makes for cakes with a crispy exterior and soft interior. Just one caution: the cakes are delicate, so be sure to flip them gently. I like to serve these in pita bread or on toast, with slices of fresh tomato and a handful of microgreens or sprouts—perhaps with a dollop of Spicy Harissa Mayonnaise (page 37) too.

---

1. If you'd like to bake the quinoa cakes rather than fry them, preheat the oven to 375°F (190°C). Line a baking sheet with parchment paper.

2. Heat the olive oil in a medium saucepan. Add the onion and garlic and sauté until tender, about 5 minutes. Add the zucchini and sauté until the zucchini is cooked through and the onion is translucent. Season to taste with salt and pepper.

3. Put the pumpkin seeds and ¾ teaspoon salt in a food processor and pulse until finely ground. Add the chickpeas, quinoa, dill, oregano, paprika, mustard, and lemon juice and pulse to combine. Then process until the mixture comes together and the chickpeas are mostly broken down but some texture remains. Drizzle in water as needed to achieve this consistency, and stop occasionally to scrape down the sides of the work bowl.

4. Transfer to a large bowl. Add the zucchini mixture and mix with your hands until evenly combined. Taste and adjust the seasonings as desired. Shape the mixture into 6 patties.

5. Bake the patties on the lined baking sheet for 10 minutes, then flip and bake for 15 minutes longer, until they are lightly browning. Alternatively, heat about a tablespoon of olive oil in a skillet over medium heat. Cook the cakes until golden brown, about 5 minutes on each side.

6. Stored in a covered container, the cakes will keep for 3 days in the fridge or 4 weeks in the freezer.

## The Best Way to Cook Quinoa

It's best to rinse quinoa before cooking; otherwise, it can be somewhat bitter. Quinoa is a small grain, so put it in a fine-mesh sieve and rinse until the water runs clear. Shake the quinoa dry, then put it in a saucepan. Stir in 2 cups (475ml) of water for each cup (170g) of quinoa. Bring to a boil over medium-high heat, stir, then turn down the heat to maintain a simmer. Cover and cook for 15 to 20 minutes, until all the water has been absorbed. Turn off the heat, fluff the quinoa with a fork, then cover the pot again and allow the quinoa to sit for 10 to 15 minutes before using in a recipe or serving. As for yield, for each cup (185g) of cooked quinoa required, use ⅓ cup (55g) of the grain.

# Smoky Tempeh and Hummus Sandwiches

SERVES 4

**Smoky Tempeh**

2 tablespoons tamari

1 tablespoon apple cider vinegar

1 tablespoon maple syrup or agave nectar

1 teaspoon olive oil

1 teaspoon smoked paprika

8 ounces (225g) tempeh, sliced in ¼-inch (6mm) strips

**Hummus**

1½ to 2 cups (250 to 330g) cooked chickpeas (see page 101)

¼ cup (60g) tahini

¼ cup (60ml) freshly squeezed lemon juice

1 clove garlic, minced

½ teaspoon salt

¼ cup (60ml) water, plus more if needed

½ teaspoon smoked paprika

1 tablespoon olive oil

8 slices crusty whole grain bread

1 cup (100g) pea shoots

Sandwiches don't get any better than this: salty, smoky tempeh meets creamy, paprika-infused hummus, with crisp green pea shoots for a bright, refreshing flavor. (If you can't get pea shoots, any type of sprout—or even a handful of fresh arugula—is a good alternative.) As for the bread, something grainy and dense is what I reach for, but your favorite sandwich loaf will do. If you're packing a lunch, keep all the components separate until it's time to eat; this will ensure that the pea shoots stay crunchy and the bread doesn't get soggy. Stored separately in the fridge, the tempeh and hummus will each keep for about 5 days.

---

1. To make the tempeh, put the tamari, vinegar, maple syrup, olive oil, and paprika in a small bowl or measuring cup and whisk until well blended. Put the tempeh in an 8-inch (20cm) square baking pan. Pour in the marinade and gently turn the tempeh until evenly coated. Cover and refrigerate for 3 to 8 hours.

2. If you'd like to bake the tempeh rather than fry it, preheat the oven to 350°F (175°C). Line a baking sheet with parchment paper. Spread the tempeh on the lined baking sheet and bake for 25 to 30 minutes, flipping the strips halfway through the baking time. Alternatively, heat a few teaspoons of olive oil in a large skillet over medium-high heat and fry the tempeh until golden on both sides.

3. To make the hummus, put the chickpeas, tahini, lemon juice, garlic, and salt in a food processor and pulse a few times to combine. With the motor running, drizzle in the water in a thin stream, stopping often to scrape down the sides of the work bowl, until the hummus has a thick and creamy texture that's easy to spread, but not liquidy. Once the texture is to your liking, add the paprika and, with the motor running, drizzle in the olive oil.

4. To assemble the sandwiches, toast the bread. For each sandwich, spread ¼ to ⅓ cup (60 to 80ml) of hummus on one slice of bread. Top with one-quarter of the tempeh slices and one-quarter of the pea shoots, then put another slice of bread on top.

# Lentil Sloppy Joes

SERVES 6

2 tablespoons olive oil

1 cup (160g) chopped white or yellow onion

1 green or red bell pepper, seeded and chopped

1 clove garlic, minced

2 teaspoons chili powder

1 teaspoon dry mustard

½ teaspoon smoked paprika

2¼ cups (450g) cooked brown or green lentils (see page 71)

1 (14.5-ounce/411g) can crushed tomatoes, preferably fire-roasted

3 tablespoons tomato paste

1 tablespoon brown sugar or maple syrup

1 tablespoon apple cider vinegar

¼ teaspoon salt

¼ teaspoon pepper

½ cup (120ml) vegetable broth, or as needed

6 hamburger buns, preferably whole grain or sprouted grain

Optional toppings, such as hot sauce, sriracha sauce, sliced pickles, sliced onions, sauerkraut, coleslaw, or avocado slices

Many vegan sloppy Joes are made with tofu, which in my view can be too moist, resulting in sandwiches that are a little *too* sloppy. Lentils are an ideal alternative: they absorb a lot of flavor and create a mixture that holds together just enough. Plus, they cook quickly. These sloppy Joes have an authentic flavor, thanks to a tangy mixture of smoked paprika, mustard, and tomatoes. Serve them on whole grain buns with any—or all—of the toppings mentioned below.

---

1. Heat the olive oil in a large pot over medium heat. Add the onion and bell pepper and sauté until the onion is tender and translucent, about 8 minutes. Add the garlic, chili powder, dry mustard, and paprika and sauté until the garlic is quite fragrant, 1 to 2 minutes.

2. Stir in the lentils, tomatoes, tomato paste, brown sugar, vinegar, salt, and pepper. Cook, stirring occasionally, until everything is hot, then decrease the heat to medium-low. Add the broth as needed to prevent sticking and achieve the desired consistency. Cook, stirring frequently, until thickened to your liking, 15 to 20 minutes. (I like thick sloppy Joes, but you may like 'em sloppier!) Taste and adjust the seasonings as desired.

3. Let cool for a few minutes, then serve sandwiched in the buns with whatever toppings you desire.

# Tempeh Kebabs with Barbecue Sauce

SERVES 4

**Barbecue Sauce**

1 (15-ounce/426g) can tomato sauce

2 tablespoons olive oil

2 tablespoons tamari

2 tablespoons maple syrup

1 tablespoon blackstrap molasses

1 tablespoon apple cider vinegar

1 teaspoon smoked paprika

1 teaspoon dried oregano

1 teaspoon chili powder

Pinch of red pepper flakes

**Kebabs**

1 pound (450g) tempeh, cut into 1½-inch (4cm) pieces

1 large red bell pepper, cut into 1½-inch (4cm) pieces

1 large zucchini, cut into 1½-inch (4cm) pieces

1 large white or yellow onion, cut into 1½-inch (4cm) pieces

8 ounces (225g) white mushrooms

I love tofu as much as the next gal, but I'm more partial to the nutty taste and dense texture of tempeh. All too often, tempeh is relegated to a supporting role, usually as one of many ingredients in a stir-fry or curry dish. Here, it's given a rightful chance to shine, accented with a sweet, tangy barbecue sauce that contrasts beautifully with the earthy taste of tempeh. If you don't have access to a grill, you can cook the kebabs in a grill pan.

---

1. To make the barbecue sauce, whisk all the ingredients together.

2. To marinate and cook the kebabs, pour the sauce into a 9-inch (23cm) square pan or a 9 by 13-inch (23 by 33cm) pan. Add the tempeh, bell pepper, zucchini, onion, and mushrooms and stir gently until evenly coated. Cover and refrigerate for 2 to 12 hours.

3. Thread the tempeh and vegetables onto skewers, alternating ingredients. Reserve any remaining sauce for basting and serving.

4. Prepare a medium-hot grill. Place the skewers on the grate and cook, turning and basting occasionally, for 7 to 10 minutes, until the vegetables are tender and everything is browning. If using a grill pan, cook over medium-high heat, turning occasionally, until the vegetables are tender and everything is browning, 8 to 10 minutes. Serve immediately.

### Tempeh vs. Tofu

You may wonder when it's better to use tofu versus tempeh. In most cases, it comes down to personal preference. However, I do like to use tofu in any recipe that calls for large pieces, since tempeh tends to break apart more readily. (It's simply easier to slice and marinate slabs of tofu.) Tempeh and tofu can be used interchangeably in stir-fries, but you may find that you prefer tempeh in sandwiches because its texture holds up well in packed lunches.

# Roasted Ratatouille

SERVES 4 TO 6

1¼ pounds (570g) Roma tomatoes, chopped

12 ounces (340g) eggplant (about 1 small), chopped into 1-inch (2.5cm) pieces and sprinkled with salt

12 ounces (340g) zucchini (about 2 small), chopped into 1-inch (2.5cm) pieces

2 red bell peppers, seeded and coarsely chopped

1 yellow or white onion, chopped

1 shallot, thinly sliced

4 cloves garlic, minced

3 cups cooked chickpeas (500g) or white beans (540g); see tip below

¼ cup (60ml) olive oil

2 tablespoon balsamic vinegar

2 teaspoons chopped fresh thyme

1¼ teaspoons salt

Pepper

¼ cup (10g) thinly sliced fresh basil, for garnish

Traditional ratatouille can be a little high maintenance: it simmers on the stovetop for an hour or longer and often requires adding specific vegetables at specific times. In this recipe, you simply mix everything together and roast it all at once. Chickpeas add substance and a chewy texture, promoting it from side dish status to the main event. You can serve it over brown rice or quinoa or on toast. For that matter, it's also an excellent chunky pasta sauce.

1. Preheat the oven to 400°F (200°C).

2. In a large roasting pan or casserole, combine the tomatoes, eggplant, zucchini, bell peppers, onion, shallot, garlic, and chickpeas. Stir well.

3. In a small bowl or measuring cup, whisk together the olive oil, vinegar, thyme, and salt until well blended. Drizzle evenly over the vegetables, then stir until all the ingredients are evenly coated. Season with pepper.

4. Bake for 20 minutes, then stir well. Bake for 20 to 30 minutes longer, until the vegetables are all very tender and the tomatoes and peppers have released their juices.

5. Taste and adjust the seasonings as desired. Serve garnished with the basil.

## The Best Way to Cook Beans

Home-cooked beans are almost always more tender and flavorful than canned (and they're not labor-intensive—promise!).

In the evening, put 2 cups (about 380g) of dried beans in a large pot and add water to cover by about 3 inches (7.5cm). The next day, drain well, then return the beans to the pot. Add fresh water—again, enough to cover them by about 3 inches (7.5cm).

Put the pot over high heat and bring to a boil. Decrease the heat to maintain a simmer, cover, and cook, stirring occasionally, until tender. Be sure to taste a few beans to make sure they're all cooked evenly. Most beans need to simmer for 1 to 2 hours; chickpeas usually take just over 1 hour. They'll keep in a covered container for 4 days in the fridge or 2 months in the freezer.

Generally, 1 cup (about 190g) of dried beans makes 2½ cups (about 440g) of cooked beans. For chickpeas, the yield is closer to 2 cups (330g).

# Kabocha Squash and Tofu Curry

SERVES 4

2 tablespoons coconut oil

1 white or yellow onion, chopped

1 clove garlic, minced

1 tablespoon minced fresh ginger

3 tablespoons red curry paste

1 tablespoon sugar, or 1 to 2 tablespoons agave nectar or maple syrup

1 (13.5-ounce/400ml) can coconut milk

2/3 cup (160ml) vegetable broth, plus more if needed

1 tablespoon tamari, plus more if desired

1 pound (450g) kabocha squash, peeled and cut into 1 1/2-inch (4cm) chunks (about 1/2 large squash, or 1 small squash)

1 green or red bell pepper, seeded and chopped

1 pound (450g) extra-firm tofu, cut into 1 1/2-inch (4cm) cubes

1 tablespoon freshly squeezed lime juice, plus more if desired

1/3 cup (13g) chopped fresh cilantro

Lime wedges, for serving

It wasn't until I went vegan that I realized how easy it can be to make delicious curries at home. All it takes is a can of coconut milk, some vegetables, and a good curry paste. I love the dense texture of kabocha squash paired with the tenderness of the tofu—the two meld together as they simmer gently in a fragrant, spicy broth. However, feel free to substitute butternut squash or sweet potatoes if kabocha squash is hard to come by. The recipe is great over most any cooked grain, and even over Asian noodles.

———————————————————————

1. Heat the coconut oil in a large pot or wok over medium heat. Add the onion and sauté until tender and translucent, about 8 minutes. Add the garlic and ginger and sauté until fragrant, about 1 minute. Add the curry paste and sugar and stir until evenly incorporated.

2. Whisk in the coconut milk, broth, and tamari. Stir in the kabocha squash, bell pepper, and tofu and bring to a simmer. Adjust the heat to maintain a simmer and cook, stirring occasionally, until the squash is tender, 30 to 35 minutes. As the curry cooks, stir in more broth to prevent sticking or to achieve the desired consistency.

3. Stir in the lime juice and remove from the heat. Taste and adjust the seasonings, perhaps adding more tamari or lime juice. Serve topped with the cilantro, with the lime wedges alongside for squeezing.

# Eggplant Tagine with Millet and Preserved Lemon

SERVES 4

### Tagine

2 tablespoons olive oil

1 white onion, diced

3 cloves garlic, minced

2 teaspoons minced fresh ginger

1 teaspoon paprika, preferably smoked

½ teaspoon ground cumin

½ teaspoon ground turmeric

1¼ pounds (570g) eggplant, cut into ½-inch (1.3cm) cubes

1¼ cups (260g) chopped roasted red bell peppers (homemade or store-bought)

1 cup (165g) cooked chickpeas (see page 101)

⅓ cup (45g) green olives, halved

4 cups (950ml) vegetable broth

1 tablespoon freshly squeezed lemon juice

¼ teaspoon salt

### Millet

1 cup (200g) millet

2 cups (475ml) vegetable broth

¼ teaspoon salt

2 tablespoons finely chopped preserved lemon

In this fragrant twist on a traditional Moroccan dish, tender eggplant and sweet bell peppers contrast with salty green olives and tart preserved lemon. Leftover tagine will keep for at least 4 days in the fridge and it freezes well. Although it pairs nicely with millet, feel free to serve it over other grains.

---

1. To make the tagine, heat the olive oil in a large pot over medium heat. Add the onion and sauté until translucent, about 8 minutes. Add the garlic, ginger, paprika, cumin, and turmeric and sauté until very fragrant, 1 to 2 minutes, adding a few splashes of water as needed to prevent sticking.

2. Add the eggplant, roasted peppers, chickpeas, and olives and stir until evenly coated with the spices. Stir in the broth and bring to a boil. Decrease the heat to a simmer and cook, stirring occasionally, until the eggplant is very soft, about 20 minutes. Stir in the lemon juice and salt.

3. Meanwhile, make the millet. Put a large, dry saucepan over medium heat. Once it's hot, pour in the millet and cook, stirring constantly, until golden brown and fragrant, about 4 minutes; a few seeds may pop up as you toast the millet. Stir in the broth and salt and bring to a boil. Decrease the heat to a simmer, cover, and cook until the millet has absorbed all the liquid, 20 to 25 minutes. Let sit for about 10 minutes, then fluff with a fork.

4. Serve the tagine over the millet and sprinkle with the preserved lemon.

## Give Millet a Chance

Millet—a small, round grain that most of us recognize as a common bird seed ingredient—doesn't get as much love as it should. It has a mildly sweet flavor and a texture that's not as light as quinoa but not as dense as rice, making it a good option for a wide range of recipes. Toasting millet first adds a nutty flavor to what can otherwise be a very neutrally flavored grain. If you'll be using it for a sweet dish, such as a breakfast porridge, substitute water for the broth. Just-cooked millet is delicious when fluffed and eaten warm. The only downside to millet is that leftovers tend to get quite dry quickly, so it's best to cook only as much as you'll use.

# Cauliflower and Oyster Mushroom Tacos

SERVES 4

1 head cauliflower, cut into small florets (6 to 8 cups/ 600 to 800g)

4 tablespoons (60ml) olive oil

1 tablespoon chili powder

1 tablespoon smoked paprika

1 teaspoon ground coriander

½ teaspoon ground cumin

Pinch of red pepper flakes

Salt and pepper

1 cup (115g) thinly sliced Vidalia or Spanish onion

1 large or 2 small poblano chiles, thinly sliced

½ cup (75g) chopped red bell pepper

1 clove garlic, minced

6 ounces (170g) oyster mushrooms, thinly sliced

2 teaspoons freshly squeezed lime juice

8 (6-inch/15cm) crisp corn tortillas

½ cup (20g) chopped fresh cilantro, for garnish

A lot of vegan tacos are filled with rice, beans, or faux meat, but vegetables can provide plenty of substance and flavor all on their own. In this recipe, spice-rubbed, crispy roasted cauliflower meets chewy, tender sautéed mushrooms, and the result is a satisfying contrast of textures and flavors. Don't be afraid to slightly char the cauliflower; that will just give it an even better flavor—trust me on this one. The garnish of cilantro complements the other flavors perfectly, but feel free to use different toppings, such as salsa, guacamole, sliced avocado, or hot sauce.

---

1. Preheat the oven to 425°F (220°C).

2. In a large bowl, toss the cauliflower florets with 2 tablespoons of the olive oil until evenly coated. Sprinkle with the chili powder, paprika, coriander, cumin, red pepper flakes, and a generous pinch of salt. Toss again until the cauliflower is evenly coated. Spread the cauliflower on a rimmed baking sheet.

3. Bake for 20 minutes, until crispy.

4. Heat the remaining 2 tablespoons of olive oil in a large skillet over medium heat. Add the onion, poblano, and red bell pepper and sauté until the onion is tender and a bit golden, about 15 minutes. Add the garlic and sauté for another minute. Stir in the mushrooms, then season with salt and pepper. Cook until the mushrooms are tender and crispy (5 to 8 minutes). Remove from the heat and stir in the lime juice. Taste and adjust the seasonings as desired.

5. For each taco, put ¼ cup (60ml) of the mushroom mixture in a tortilla. Top with some of the roasted cauliflower and a tablespoonful of cilantro.

# Mushroom, Chard, and Quinoa Enchiladas

SERVES 6

## Sauce

1 tablespoon olive oil

1 cup (160g) diced onion

2 cloves garlic, minced

1½ teaspoons chili powder

1 teaspoon ground cumin

1 teaspoon chopped oregano

1 (14.5-ounce/411g) can diced tomatoes

1 teaspoon maple syrup

⅓ cup (80ml) water

Salt

## Enchiladas

1 tablespoon olive oil

1 small yellow onion, chopped

2 cloves garlic, minced

12 ounces (340g) cremini mushrooms, chopped

3 cups (225g) chopped Swiss chard

½ cup (75g) diced fresh poblano chiles

½ teaspoon ground cumin

¼ teaspoon salt

1½ cups (255g) cooked black beans (see page 101)

1½ cups (280g) cooked quinoa (see page 93)

10 (6-inch/15cm) whole wheat or corn tortillas

½ cup (20g) chopped fresh cilantro

These enchiladas are the epitome of crowd-pleasing cold-weather fare. The sweet, gently spiced red sauce is the perfect complement to the filling: a richly textured combination of quinoa, black beans, and winter vegetables. Because preparing the components is somewhat involved, I've called for a simple garnish of chopped cilantro. But truth be told, I like to top these enchiladas with a drizzle of Savory Cashew Cream (page 137)—a spin on sour cream—and a shower of fresh parsley or cilantro.

1. To make the sauce, heat the olive oil in a medium saucepan over medium heat. Add the onion and sauté for 3 minutes. Add the garlic and sauté until the onion is tender and translucent, about 8 minutes. Stir in the chili powder, cumin, oregano, tomatoes, and maple syrup.

2. Transfer to a blender or food processor and process until smooth, adding the water as needed to adjust the consistency as you wish. Season with salt to taste.

3. Preheat the oven to 350°F (175°C).

4. To make the enchiladas, heat the olive oil in a large pot over medium heat. Add the onion and garlic and sauté until the onion is tender and translucent, about 8 minutes. Add the mushrooms and sauté until they release their liquids and the liquid evaporates. Stir in the Swiss chard and chiles and cook, stirring occasionally, until the chard wilts slightly. Stir in the cumin, salt, beans, and quinoa and continue to cook, stirring occasionally, until heated through.

5. To assemble and bake the enchiladas, spread a thin layer of the sauce in the bottom of a 7 by 11-inch (18 by 28cm) baking pan. Put about ¼ cup of the filling in the center of a tortilla and roll the tortilla up around the filling. Place it in the baking pan, seam side down. Repeat with the remaining tortillas and filling. Spread the remaining sauce evenly over the top.

6. Bake for 25 minutes, until the edges of the tortillas are crisp. Top the enchiladas with chopped cilantro.

# Desserts

# Ginger Roasted Pears with Vanilla Cream

SERVES 4

4 medium to large Bosc pears, halved and cored

1 tablespoon freshly squeezed lemon juice

⅓ cup (65g) brown sugar

2 tablespoons grated fresh ginger

Sweet Cashew Cream (page 137), for serving

Poached pears are a classic dessert option, but I'm partial to roasting pears, as it brings out their natural sweetness and creates a meltingly tender texture. In this recipe, they're infused with brown sugar and ginger, so they have the flavors of a fruit tart or pie while requiring only a fraction of the work. The vanilla-spiked cashew cream is a simple accompaniment, but it makes for a gorgeous and sophisticated dessert. Just one heads-up: although the cashew cream is a breeze to prepare, the cashews must soak for at least 3 hours before making it, so plan ahead.

---

1. Preheat the oven to 375°F (190°C).

2. Arrange the pear halves in a single layer in a baking pan, cut side up. Drizzle the pears with the lemon juice, then sprinkle the sugar and ginger evenly over them. Pour a small amount of water (just a few tablespoons) into the pan.

3. Bake for 25 to 30 minutes, until the tops are golden, occasionally basting them with the juices they've released. Flip the pears over and bake for 10 to 15 minutes longer.

4. For each serving, place 2 pear halves, cut side up, on a plate. If any juices remain in the baking pan, drizzle them over the pears. Top each serving with a generous dollop of the cashew cream.

# Banana Chia Pudding

SERVES 4

3 cups unsweetened almond milk, homemade (page 134) or store-bought, plus more as needed

2 large bananas

3 tablespoons maple syrup

1 teaspoon ground cinnamon

1 teaspoon vanilla extract, or seeds scraped from 1 vanilla bean

⅛ teaspoon salt

¾ cup (120g) chia seeds

Fresh berries, for garnish (optional)

Mint sprigs, for garnish (optional)

As if by magic, chia seeds plump up when soaked in liquid, creating a quick and easy pudding (this also makes them great for thickening smoothies). They have a neutral flavor, which means that it's easy to adapt chia puddings to your taste. I like to add cocoa powder, fresh berries, and dried fruit; you could also blend peaches or other fruit into the almond milk before adding it to the seeds. And since chia pudding requires overnight preparation, it's also a terrific make-ahead breakfast that will satisfy cravings for something sweet yet healthful. The bananas will brown slightly overnight, but this won't affect their flavor, so don't be put off. Just remember that riper bananas will make for a sweeter, softer pudding.

---

1. Put the almond milk, bananas, maple syrup, cinnamon, vanilla, and salt in a blender and process until smooth.

2. Put the chia seeds in a medium bowl. Pour in the banana mixture and stir well. Let sit for 5 minutes, then stir again. Let sit for another 10 minutes, then give it another good stir; at this point the chia seeds should be getting plump and the mixture should start to resemble a loose tapioca pudding.

3. Cover and refrigerate for 8 hours. Before serving, check the consistency; if it's too thick, stir in more almond milk to achieve the desired consistency. Serve garnished with fresh berries or a sprig of mint. Stored in an airtight container in the fridge, the pudding will keep for 3 to 4 days.

# Chai-Spiced Bread Pudding

SERVES 6

⅓ cup (80ml) melted coconut oil, plus more for coating the pan

3 cups almond milk, homemade (page 134) or store-bought

1¼ cups (310g) pitted medjool dates, soaked in warm water for at least 1 hour and drained

2 tablespoons ground flaxseeds

1 teaspoon ground cinnamon

¾ teaspoon ground ginger

½ teaspoon ground nutmeg

½ teaspoon ground cardamom

1½ teaspoons vanilla extract

1 large French baguette (about 7 ounces/200g), at least 1 day old, cut into cubes

1 cup (145g) raisins

Caramelly medjool dates makes this bread pudding richer and more complex than if it were sweetened with regular sugar, and the hint of coconut oil so nicely complements the array of spices. As a bonus, this easy and healthful dessert can double as breakfast if you're hankering for something sweet.

_____

1. Preheat the oven to 350°F (175°C). Coat an 8-inch (20cm) square baking pan with coconut oil.

2. Put the almond milk, dates, coconut oil, ground flaxseeds, cinnamon, ginger, nutmeg, cardamom, and vanilla in a blender and process until very smooth.

3. Put the bread and raisins in a large bowl. Pour in the date mixture and toss gently until evenly combined. Let the bread soak up the liquid for about 10 minutes. Transfer to the prepared pan and spread everything evenly.

4. Bake for 30 to 40 minutes, until the top is golden brown. Let cool slightly before serving.

## Date Paste: Your New Favorite Sweetener

Date paste is slightly less sweet than agave nectar or maple syrup, but it can be used almost interchangeably with either (substitute 1¼ parts date paste for every 1 part traditional sweetener). Soak 1 cup (250g) pitted and packed medjool dates in warm water for a few hours, then drain and blend with about ½ cup (120ml) of water and a small pinch of salt. Use it in baking, in puddings, on top of tarts or pies, or drizzled over warm porridge or oatmeal.

# Blackberry Coconut Ice Cream

SERVES 4

2 (13.5-ounce/400ml) cans full-fat coconut milk, chilled

¾ cup (150g) sugar

Seeds scraped from 1 vanilla bean

Generous pinch of salt

1 cup (150g) fresh blackberries

Nearly all ice cream recipes start with a custard before freezing, but thanks to full-fat coconut milk, you can skip that step entirely, streamlining the process while still creating an ice cream that's rich and smooth. Just blend coconut milk with vanilla, sugar, salt, and, in this recipe, fresh blackberries, then let the mixture churn in an ice cream maker until thick and creamy. The basic formula here can be used as a blank canvas for many flavor variations: try lime juice and zest, strawberries, cocoa powder and dark chocolate chunks, or a ribbon of peanut butter.

---

1. The day before you make the ice cream, refrigerate the ice cream maker basin according to the manufacturer's instructions.

2. When the basin is ready, put all the ingredients in a blender and process until totally smooth, 1 to 3 minutes.

3. Transfer the mixture to the ice cream maker; or, if it warmed up during blending, you may want to cool it down in the fridge first. Let churn for 20 to 25 minutes, or however long the manufacturer's instructions indicate.

4. Transfer to a freezer-safe container and freeze for a few hours before serving.

# Cranberry Pistachio Biscotti

MAKES 15 BISCOTTI

2 cups (250g) unbleached all-purpose flour

1½ teaspoons baking powder

¼ teaspoon salt

3 tablespoons warm water

1½ teaspoons Egg Replacer (page 133)

⅓ cup (80ml) unsweetened almond milk, homemade (page 134) or store-bought

½ cup (110g) coconut oil, cold or at cool room temperature

¾ cup (150g) sugar

1 teaspoon almond extract

1 teaspoon vanilla extract

½ cup (60g) chopped pistachios

½ cup (60g) dried cranberries

While I typically use ground flaxseeds mixed with water as a vegan egg replacement, that can be too dense for delicate baked goods like cakes or cookies. Those are the times to reach for the alternative egg replacer called for in this recipe. It offers leavening power without weighing down a dough or batter, as evidenced by these light, crispy biscotti. They're great to have around for snacking, and the bright pop of cranberries makes them a perfect holiday gift.

1. Preheat the oven to 350°F (175°C). Line a baking sheet with parchment paper.

2. In a medium bowl, whisk together the flour, baking powder, and salt.

3. In a small bowl or measuring cup, whisk together the water and egg replacer. Stir in the almond milk.

4. Using an electric mixer, beat the coconut oil, sugar, and almond and vanilla extracts together until fluffy, 2 to 3 minutes. Add the almond milk mixture. With the mixer running, gradually add the flour mixture and mix just until incorporated. Add the pistachios and dried cranberries and stir until evenly incorporated.

5. Put the dough on the lined baking sheet and shape it into a log about 1 inch (2.5cm) tall, 8 to 9 inches (20 to 23cm) long, and 5 inches (13cm) wide. Bake for 30 to 35 minutes, until the dough has risen a bit and is fairly solid.

6. Remove from the oven and increase the oven temperature to 375°F (190°C). As soon as the log is cool enough to handle, cut it into ¾-inch (2cm) slices and lay the slices on the baking sheet.

7. Bake for 20 to 25 minutes, until dry and lightly golden. Transfer to a wire rack and let cool before serving.

8. Stored in an airtight container at room temperature, the biscotti will keep for 1 week.

# Perfect Pumpkin Pie

SERVES 8

## Crust

1¼ cups (160g) unbleached all-purpose flour

1½ teaspoons sugar

½ teaspoon salt

⅓ cup (80g) coconut oil, cold or at cool room temperature

¼ cup (60ml) ice water, plus more as needed

## Filling

2½ cups (610g) pumpkin puree

1 cup (130g) cashew pieces, soaked in water for at least 3 hours and drained

¾ cup (150g) sugar

2 tablespoons tapioca starch (sometimes sold as tapioca flour)

1 teaspoon ground cinnamon

½ teaspoon ground ginger

¼ teaspoon ground nutmeg

Pinch of ground cloves

2 tablespoons blackstrap molasses

1 teaspoon vanilla extract

As it turns out, everyone's favorite holiday dessert holds up just fine without eggs, milk, or butter. Vegan pumpkin pie can include silken tofu or vegan cream cheese for creaminess in the filling, but another alternative (and my favorite) is to use cashews. You'll be amazed at how similar the texture is to a traditional custard. As for the crust, versatile and healthful coconut oil saves the day, making for a pastry that's fragrant, buttery, and super flaky. The pie can be prepared up to 2 days in advance, and it's sure to win over even the pickiest pumpkin pie lovers.

---

1. First, make the crust. To use a food processor, put the flour, sugar, and salt in the processor bowl and pulse to combine. Add the coconut oil and pulse until the mixture is crumbly and a bit of it sticks together when squeezed. With the motor running, slowly drizzle in the ice water, using just enough to bring the dough together. It's fine to have some crumbs—that makes for a good, flaky crust—but the dough should be easy to shape into a unified mass.

2. To mix the dough by hand, whisk together the flour, sugar, and salt in a large bowl. Cut the coconut oil into small pieces and work it into the flour with dry hands. Add the water, using just enough to bring the dough together, and knead until it can be shaped into a unified mass.

3. Transfer the dough to a lightly floured work surface. If you're not ready to use the crust, shape it into a disk, then wrap it in plastic wrap and put it in the fridge. (For longer storage, put the wrapped dough in a freezer bag and freeze for up to 8 weeks.) If you've refrigerated or frozen the dough, remove it well before rolling it out so it can warm to room temperature to ease rolling.

4. Working on a floured work surface, roll the dough out to form a large circle about 10 inches (25cm) in diameter, lightly dusting the work surface, dough, or rolling pin with flour as needed to prevent sticking. Carefully transfer to an 8-inch (20cm) pie plate. Don't worry if the crust tears a bit; once it's in the pan, you can push the dough back together with your fingertips. Trim away any excess dough and squeeze the dough along the rim to make a pretty fluted pattern. Refrigerate the crust while you prepare the filling.

5. Preheat the oven to 350°F (175°C).

6. To make the filling, put all the ingredients in a food processor and process until very smooth, stopping occasionally to scrape down the sides of the work bowl. It should be quite thick, but if it's too thick to process well, drizzle in a bit of water or nondairy milk.

7. To assemble and bake the pie, spoon the filling into the crust and smooth the top. Bake for 35 to 40 minutes, until the edges of the crust are golden brown and the filling is dark. Let cool briefly before slicing and serving.

8. Stored covered in the fridge, leftovers will keep for up to 5 days.

# Raw Citrus Cheesecake

SERVES 12

## Crust

1 1/2 cups almonds (210g)
or walnuts (150g)

Pinch of salt

1 2/3 cups (410g) pitted
medjool dates

## Filling

3 cups (390g) cashews,
soaked in water for at least
3 hours and drained

2/3 cup (160ml) melted
coconut oil

1/2 cup (120ml) agave nectar

2 tablespoons finely grated
orange zest

1/4 cup (60ml) freshly
squeezed orange juice

1 teaspoon finely grated
lemon zest

2 tablespoons freshly
squeezed lemon juice

Seeds scraped from 1 vanilla
bean, or 2 teaspoons vanilla
extract

1/4 teaspoon salt

Finely grated lemon zest
(optional), for garnish

I'm a big fan of raw desserts, which are often born from a combination of dried fruits and nuts—both soaked and unsoaked. These ingredients have the potential to be incredibly rich and brightly flavored. As an added bonus, there's no need to turn the oven on. Don't be put off by the fact that this sweet and citrusy cheesecake makes so many servings. Let's be honest: you'll probably eat it for breakfast—which is perfectly okay.

1. To make the crust, put the almonds and salt in a food processor and pulse until coarsely ground. Add the dates and process until the mixture is uniform and a bit of it sticks together when squeezed. Press the mixture evenly into the bottom of a 9-inch (23cm) round springform pan.

2. To make the filling, put all the ingredients in a blender (preferably a high-speed blender) or food processor and process until silky smooth, stopping occasionally to scrape down the sides of the blender jar or work bowl.

3. To assemble and chill the cheesecake, pour the filling over the crust and smooth the top. Refrigerate for at least 2 hours before slicing and serving. If you like, garnish the cheesecake with additional lemon zest.

4. Stored in a covered container in the fridge, any leftovers will keep for 1 week.

# Double-Chocolate Brownies

MAKES 6 LARGE BROWNIES OR 9 SMALLER BROWNIES

2 tablespoons lukewarm water

1 tablespoon ground flaxseeds

1½ cups (190g) unbleached all-purpose flour

1½ cups (300g) sugar

½ cup (40g) unsweetened cocoa powder

1 teaspoon baking powder

¾ teaspoon salt

1 tablespoon instant espresso powder

1¼ cups (300ml) unsweetened nondairy milk, homemade (pages 133 and 134) or store-bought

½ cup (120ml) canola oil

2 teaspoons vanilla extract

½ cup (85g) chocolate chips

½ cup (50g) walnuts, chopped

People often ask me if chocolate is vegan-friendly, and I always reply that if it weren't, I'd be one grief-stricken vegan! The good news is, a lot of bittersweet or dark chocolate is dairy-free. But do read the ingredients even for these; sometimes milk or milk powder is included. Once you've gotten your hands on some vegan chocolate chips, whip up these dense, chewy, walnut-studded vegan brownies. Instant espresso powder heightens the chocolate flavor and gives the brownies a wonderful mocha taste.

1. Preheat the oven to 350°F (175°C) and oil an 8-inch (20cm) square baking pan.

2. In a small bowl or measuring cup, whisk together the water and ground flaxseeds and let sit until thick.

3. In a large bowl, whisk together the flour, sugar, cocoa powder, baking powder, salt, and espresso powder.

4. In a medium bowl, whisk together the nondairy milk, oil, vanilla, and flaxseed mixture. Add to the flour mixture, along with the chocolate chips and walnuts, and stir just until combined. Pour the batter into the prepared pan and smooth the top.

5. Bake for 45 to 55 minutes, until a toothpick inserted into the center comes out clean.

6. Let cool for 20 to 30 minutes before cutting into squares and serving.

## Choosing Sugar

You may be surprised to hear that a great deal of the sugar sold in the United States isn't vegan. Bone char—charcoal made from pulverized animal bones—is frequently used in the refining process for conventional cane sugar. For this reason, most vegans avoid conventional white and brown sugars. All organic sugar (white, brown, and confectioners') is made without bone char and is therefore vegan, as are evaporated cane juice, unbleached cane sugar, Demerara sugar, and liquid sweeteners like maple syrup and agave nectar.

# Chocolate Cake with Chocolate Filling and Ganache

SERVES 10 TO 12

## Cake

3 cups (375g) unbleached all-purpose flour

2/3 cup (60g) unsweetened cocoa powder

2 teaspoons baking soda

3/4 teaspoon salt

2 cups (475ml) unsweetened nondairy milk, homemade (pages 133 and 134) or store-bought

2 tablespoons apple cider vinegar

1 3/4 cups (350g) sugar

2/3 cup (160ml) melted coconut oil

2 teaspoons vanilla extract

## Filling

1 cup (245g) pumpkin puree

1/4 cup (20g) unsweetened cocoa powder

1/4 cup (60ml) maple syrup

3 tablespoons almond butter or cashew butter

## Ganache

6 ounces (170g) bittersweet chocolate, finely chopped

1/2 cup (120ml) coconut milk

2 tablespoons maple syrup

Yes, it is true: vegan chocolate cake can deliver all the flavor and satisfaction of its egg- and butter-filled cousins, as this one amply demonstrates. The "buttercream" in this recipe is an ingenious combination of pumpkin puree and almond butter. If you don't have time to bake a cake, it wouldn't be a terrible idea to make the filling anyway and eat it with a spoon.

1. Preheat the oven to 350°F (175°C). Coat two 8- or 9-inch (20 or 23cm) round springform pans with melted coconut oil.

2. To make the cake, put the flour, cocoa, baking soda, and salt in a large bowl and whisk to combine.

3. In a medium bowl, vigorously whisk together the nondairy milk and vinegar until frothy. Whisk in the sugar, oil, and vanilla. Add about one-third of the mixture to the flour mixture and stir with a spatula or whisk, or use an electric mixer on the lowest setting. Repeat, adding the remaining liquid in two more additions, mixing just until incorporated after the final addition. Pour the batter into the prepared pans.

4. Bake for about 25 minutes, until a toothpick inserted into the center comes out clean. Remove from the oven but leave the cakes in their pans and let cool completely.

5. To make the filling, process all the ingredients in a food processor.

6. To make the ganache, put the chocolate in a medium heatproof bowl. Combine the coconut milk and maple syrup in a small saucepan over medium-low heat. Cook, stirring occasionally, until just simmering. Pour over the chocolate and stir until melted. Let cool to room temperature.

7. To assemble the cake, remove the layers from their pans. Place one, top side up, on a serving platter and gently shave off the rounded top with a sharp knife. Spread all of the filling over the top. Place the other cake layer atop the filling. Pour the ganache evenly over the top and let it drizzle down the sides. Refrigerate for at least 1 hour before serving.

8. Leftovers will keep in a covered container in the fridge for up to 4 days.

# Mexican Chocolate Date Truffles

MAKES 20 TO 25 BALLS

1½ cups (about 180g) nuts

3 tablespoons unsweetened cocoa powder

¼ teaspoon salt

½ teaspoon ground chiles

Pinch of cayenne pepper

1⅔ cups (310g) pitted medjool dates

1½ teaspoons melted coconut oil

This is a perfect dessert to prepare when you're short on time and unmotivated to bake but craving chocolate (an instinct one should never ignore). Since these chewy truffles are made with little more than ground almonds, cocoa powder, and pitted medjool dates, they feel more like a rich snack than a full-on dessert, although they would be the perfect finishing touch at any meal (and make great edible gifts, too!). I love the way dried chiles and cayenne add a kick of spice and enhance the flavor of cocoa in the version below, but the variations are endless (see below). Have fun experimenting with whatever spices and dried fruits appeal to you—just be sure to keep the simple ratio of about one part nuts to one part dates.

---

1. Put the nuts, cocoa, salt, chile powder, and cayenne in a food processor and pulse a few times to break down the nuts. Add the dates and the coconut oil and process until the mixture starts to clump and a handful sticks together and holds its shape when squeezed.

2. Roll into balls about 1 inch (2.5cm) in diameter. Stored in an airtight container, the truffles will keep for 2 weeks in the fridge or 1 week at room temperature.

## For Something Different

**Key Lime Truffles** Omit the chile powder and cayenne. Add the finely grated zest and juice of 3 limes when you add the dates and coconut oil.

**Lemon Coconut Truffles** Omit the chile powder and cayenne. Add the finely grated zest and juice of 2 lemons when you add the dates and coconut oil. Roll the balls in unsweetened shredded dried coconut before serving.

**Oatmeal Raisin Truffles** Omit the chile powder and cayenne. Replace ½ cup (60g) of the nuts with ½ cup (45g) rolled oats. Once the mixture is coming together, pulse in ⅓ cup (50g) raisins and ½ teaspoon ground cinnamon.

# Basics

# Egg Replacer

MAKES 3 CUPS (710ML)

There are several ways to supply the leavening and binding qualities of eggs in vegan baking. Options include flax and chia eggs (see tip below) and certain fruits, such as ¼ cup mashed banana or applesauce per egg. But for lighter baked goods, like cookies, cakes, and biscotti, this is the egg replacer I recommend. It can be stored in an airtight container for several months at room temperature.

2 ½ cups arrowroot powder (125g), potato starch (160g), or tapioca starch (125g)

½ cup (80g) baking powder

1 tablespoon xanthan gum powder

1. Whisk together all the ingredients. Stored in an airtight container at room temperature, the egg replacer will keep for 3 months—or possibly quite a bit longer.

2. To replace 1 egg, whisk together 1½ teaspoons of the egg replacer and 3 tablespoons of warm water. Let sit for a moment, then add it to the recipe in place of the egg.

## Flax and Chia Eggs

To help bind batters for quick breads and muffins without using eggs, you can use ground flaxseeds or ground chia seeds. For each egg, whisk 1 tablespoon of ground flaxseeds or chia seeds into 3 tablespoons of warm water and let the mixture sit until it becomes thick and gelatinous. It's an inexpensive, effective binder, with the added benefit of providing uber-healthy omega-3 fatty acids.

# Oat Milk

MAKES ABOUT 3½ CUPS (830ML)

Making oat milk may take you less time than running to the store to pick some up. While it isn't quite as rich or creamy as nut milk, it's much faster to make because oats require only 1 hour of soaking. It's my emergency option when I've run out of almonds, cashews, and other nuts, because chances are I have steel-cut oats on hand. Oat milk is great in smoothies, puddings, and—not surprisingly—stirred into a bowl of warm oats or another porridge. If you'll be using the oat milk in a savory dish, omit the maple syrup and vanilla.

1 cup (180g) steel-cut oats, soaked in water for 1 hour and drained

3 cups (710ml) water

3 tablespoons maple syrup (optional)

1 teaspoon vanilla extract (optional)

⅛ teaspoon salt

1. Put all the ingredients in a blender and process until smooth. For a thicker texture, use the oat milk as is. Or, for a thinner liquid, strain it: Cover the mouth of a large container with two layers of cheesecloth, leaving a well in the cheesecloth (a new paint strainer bag or a nut milk bag, which is cheap and easy to find online, will also work well). Secure with a rubber band, then pour in the blended mixture. You may need to do this in batches, gently pushing some of the pulp to the side or spooning it out and discarding it. After pouring all of the mixture in, let it sit for about 10 minutes. Loosen the cheesecloth from the rim of the container and gently squeeze to extract as much liquid as possible.

2. Stored in an airtight container in the fridge, the oat milk will keep for 3 days. Shake well before using.

# Nut Milk

MAKES ABOUT 3 CUPS (710ML)

Homemade nut milks are undeniably the best: creamy, rich, and easy to adapt to your own tastes. If you're preparing something savory (like soup or mashed potatoes), omit the dates and vanilla. (And if you want to streamline the process, you can skip the straining step; you'll just get a thicker milk.)

While almonds are the most popular base for nut milk, you can use a wide variety of nuts and seeds, including Brazil nuts, macadamia nuts, cashews, pecans, pumpkin seeds, and even sesame seeds. Macadamias, Brazil nuts, and almonds tend to give the creamiest texture. Cashew milk is easier because it doesn't demand any straining. Seeds can be a good choice if time is limited, as they require less soaking time: 3 to 4 hours, rather than 8 to 12.

1 cup (about 120g) nuts, soaked in water for 8 to 12 hours and drained

4 cups (950ml) water

4 pitted medjool dates, or ¼ cup (60ml) maple syrup (optional)

1 teaspoon vanilla extract (optional)

Small pinch of salt

1. Put all the ingredients in a blender. Blend on high speed until completely smooth, with no pieces of nut or date visible, 2 to 3 minutes.

2. Cover the mouth of a large container with two layers of cheesecloth, leaving a well in the cheesecloth (a new paint strainer bag or a nut milk bag will also work well). Secure with a rubber band, then pour in the blended mixture. You may need to do this in batches, gently pushing some of the pulp to the side or spooning it out and discarding it. After pouring all of the mixture in, let it sit for about 10 minutes. Loosen the cheesecloth from the rim of the container and gently squeeze to extract as much liquid as possible.

3. Stored in an airtight container in the fridge, the nut milk will keep for 2 to 3 days. Shake well before using.

## Choosing the Right Nondairy Milk for the Job

For smoothies and cereals, most plant milks can be used interchangeably. For savory dishes, be sure to choose an unsweetened variety. I find that soy milk and coconut milk are best for creamy soups, while almond milk and rice milk have a smooth texture and neutral flavor that works well for most baked goods. For the creamiest texture of all, homemade nut milk can't be beat.

# Horchata

MAKES ABOUT 3½ CUPS (830ML)

Traditional horchata, a combination of nuts and rice soaked in water and blended with spices and sweeteners is often vegan as-is. It's a refreshing alternative to standard nut milk. This version calls for cashews, but you can definitely substitute almonds or use a combination of the two. The horchata makes for a lovely and lightly sweet beverage, but it also works well in smoothies or cereal.

½ cup (90g) long-grain white rice, such as basmati, rinsed

1 (3-inch/7.5cm) cinnamon stick, broken into a few pieces

1 cup (130g) cashew pieces

4 cups (950ml) water

½ cup (100g) sugar

⅛ teaspoon salt

1. Use a food processor or a high-speed blender to coarsely grind the rice and cinnamon stick. Transfer to a medium bowl or jar, add the cashews, then pour in 2 cups (475ml) of the water. Let soak for 8 to 12 hours.

2. Transfer to a blender. Add the remaining 2 cups (475ml) of water and the sugar and salt, and blend until smooth.

3. Cover the mouth of a large container with two layers of cheesecloth, leaving a well in the cheesecloth (a new paint strainer bag or a nut milk bag will also work well). Secure with a rubber band, then pour in the blended mixture. You may need to do this in batches, gently pushing some of the pulp to the side or spooning it out and discarding it. After pouring all of the mixture in, let it sit for about 10 minutes. Loosen the cheesecloth from the rim of the container and gently squeeze to extract as much liquid as possible.

4. Stored in an airtight container in the fridge, the horchata will keep for 2 to 3 days. Shake well before using.

# Herbed Cashew Cheese

MAKES ABOUT 1¼ CUPS (300ML)

Nut cheese can be made with almonds, Brazil nuts, macadamia nuts, or pine nuts, but cashews, with their buttery texture and mild taste, are perfectly suited to the task. This cashew cheese, which is soft and spreadable, is infused with herbs for a more complex flavor profile and nutritional yeast for a kick of umami. Spread it on crackers or toast or crumble it over a salad.

1½ cups (195g) cashew pieces or a combination of cashews and pine nuts, soaked in water for at least 3 hours and drained

2 tablespoons large-flake nutritional yeast

1 teaspoon salt

2 teaspoons herbes de Provence

¼ teaspoon pepper

3 tablespoons freshly squeezed lemon juice

1 clove garlic, minced

4 tablespoons (60ml) water

1. Put the cashews in a food processor or blender (preferably a high-speed blender). Add the nutritional yeast, salt, herbes de Provence, pepper, lemon juice, and garlic. Pulse a few times to break the cashews down until they have a wet, coarse, mealy texture.

2. With the motor running, drizzle in 2 tablespoons of the water. Now it's time for some kitchen intuition: keep adding water, stopping occasionally to scrape down the sides of the work bowl, until the mixture has a good consistency. It should be similar to thick hummus—a little coarse, but smooth and spreadable. You may not need all of the remaining 2 tablespoons of water. (If using a blender, start on a low speed and gradually increase to high speed as you add the water, using a plunger attachment the entire time to keep the mixture blending.)

3. Taste and adjust the seasonings as desired. Stored in a covered container in the fridge, the cheese will keep for about 5 days.

# Tofu Feta

MAKES 14 OUNCES (400G)

Here's a creative spin on feta cheese that involves marinating tofu in a tart, salty dressing. The delicious results are perfect for a Greek salad (page 63), of course, but this cheese is also excellent atop other salads, stuffed into wraps, or enjoyed as part of a meze platter.

1 (14-ounce/400g) block of tofu

¼ cup (60ml) water

¼ cup (60ml) freshly squeezed lemon juice

2½ tablespoons white miso

2 tablespoons apple cider vinegar

1 teaspoon dried oregano

1. Press the tofu for at least 1 hour (see page 137).

2. In a small bowl or measuring cup, whisk together the water, lemon juice, miso, vinegar, and oregano.

3. Cut the tofu into 1-inch (2.5cm) cubes. Place the tofu in an 8-inch (20cm) square baking pan. Pour in the marinade and gently stir until the tofu is evenly coated. Cover and refrigerate for at least 4 hours or, for optimum flavor, up to 2 days. Drain well before using. Stored in a covered container in the fridge, the feta will keep for up to 5 days.

## Getting to Know Nutritional Yeast

If you're starting to prepare more dairy-free meals, it's time to get to know nutritional yeast, lovingly called "nooch" in the vegan culinary world. It has an unmistakable cheesy flavor, making it essential in pesto (page 86), cashew cheese (see left), cheese sauce (page 82), and the like. You may even enjoy it as a condiment, sprinkled on salads or warm grains.

## Savory Cashew Cream

MAKES ABOUT 2¾ CUPS (650ML)

Cashew cream is a secret weapon of vegan cooking, supplying the creamy texture that many people fear they'll miss in vegan cuisine. Use it in place of crème fraîche, sour cream, or dairy cream; as a garnish; or as a component of baked goods, soups—including the Gingered Carrot Bisque (page 49)—and pasta sauces. As is, it's also a wonderful vegan béchamel sauce.

2 cups (260g) cashew pieces, soaked in water for at least 3 hours and drained

1 to 2 tablespoons freshly squeezed lemon juice (optional)

½ teaspoon salt (optional)

1 cup (240ml) cold water, plus more if desired

1. Put the cashews in a food processor or high-speed blender and pulse a few times to grind them up. Add the lemon juice and salt. With the motor running, drizzle in the water and process until completely smooth (which may take a few minutes), stopping occasionally to scrape down the sides of the work bowl or blender jar. Add more water for a thinner consistency, if desired; you may want it as thick as whipped cream or as thin as coconut milk, depending on how you plan to use it.

2. Stored in a covered container in the fridge, the cashew cream will keep for up to 6 days.

## Sweet Cashew Cream

MAKES ABOUT 1¾ CUPS (415ML)

With the addition of agave nectar or maple syrup, a bit of coconut oil for creaminess, and a hint of vanilla, cashew cream becomes a sweet and easy topping for fresh or cooked fruit (see the roasted pears on page 113) or any number of pies, including pumpkin pie (page 122).

1 cup (130g) cashew pieces, soaked in water for at least 3 hours and drained

¼ cup (60ml) agave nectar or maple syrup

2 tablespoons melted coconut oil

¾ cup (175ml) water

Seeds scraped from 1 vanilla bean, or 1 teaspoon vanilla extract

Small pinch of salt

1. Put the cashews in a food processor or high-speed blender and pulse a few times to grind them up. Add the agave nectar and coconut oil. With the motor running, drizzle in the water and process until completely smooth (which may take a few minutes), stopping occasionally to scrape down the sides of the work bowl or blender jar. Add more water for a thinner consistency, if desired; you may want it as thick as whipped cream or as thin as coconut milk, depending on how you plan to use it.

2. Stored in a covered container in the fridge, the cashew cream will keep for up to 6 days.

# Acknowledgments

First and foremost, a huge thank you to my Food52 family. Amanda and Merrill, thank you for championing the New Veganism column from the beginning, for teaching me how to be a stronger food writer, and for inspiring me to be a much better, smarter, happier cook. Kristen Miglore, thank you for your stewardship of this project and for supporting my recipes, week in and week out. James Ransom, thank you for making my food look so incredibly tasty. Marian Bull, thank you for helping me bring the New Veganism to life each week, for making this book so beautiful, and for sharing my passion for sweet potatoes, avocado toast, yoga, words, and—above all else—sauce. Many thanks to Erin, Allison, Lisa, and the rest of the kitchen team for their hard work, and to Sarah Jampel for her support of my column and this project.

Tremendous gratitude to Ali Slagle, Emily Timberlake, and Hannah Rahill for your insightful edits and vision. Thank you to Jasmine Star for your meticulous edits and to Emma Campion, Margaux Keres, and everyone at Ten Speed Press for your hard work on the book.

Thanks to the readers of my blog, who have cheered the New Veganism on from the very start. Thanks to all of my friends in the vegan and activist communities, who inspire me to show the world how delicious vegan fare can be.

Steven Leiser-Mitchell, thank you for your patience and support as this project came to life. Thank you for sharing food with me, for being the most enthusiastic recipe guinea pig a girl could hope for, and for liking my peach coffee cake so much. I love you.

Mom, thank you for supporting me in all of my endeavors, including this one.

Finally, a big thank you to Chloe Polemis. Chlo, our shared passion for food is a constant source of inspiration to me. Thank you for being one of the few people with whom I can spend hours discussing recipes, ingredients, restaurants, and meals. Thank you for reading my blog from the very start. Thank you for being the best. This book is dedicated to you.

# Index

Published in the United States by Ten Speed Press,
an imprint of the Crown Publishing Group, a division
of Penguin Random House LLC, New York.
www.crownpublishing.com
www.tenspeed.com

Ten Speed Press and the Ten Speed Press colophon are
registered trademarks of Penguin Random House LLC.

Library of Congress Cataloging-in-Publication Data
Hamshaw, Gena.
Food 52 vegan : 60 vegetable-driven recipes for
any kitchen / Gena Hamshaw ; photography by
James Ransom.— First edition.
    pages cm
Includes bibliographical references and index.
1.  Vegan cooking. 2.  Veganism. 3.  Cooking (Vegetables)
I. Title. II. Title: 60 vegetable-driven recipes for any kitchen.
III. Title: Food fifty-two vegan. IV. Title: Food52 vegan.
TX837.H32 2015
641.5'636—dc23

Hardcover ISBN: 978-1-60774-799-4
eBook ISBN: 978-1-60774-800-7

Printed in China

Design by Emma Campion and Margaux Keres

10 9 8 7 6 5 4 3 2 1

First Edition